Letters From Nepal

By: Douglas Deline

Douglas Deline
Inline Publishing
1183 E. Phillips Ct.
Midland, MI
48640.

ISBN: 978-0-9859128-0-2

Front Cover photo: Both the Annapurna range of the Himalayas and poinsettias were visible from October to December from my village.

Rear Cover photo: One day each week hill people bring produce such as guavas and cucumbers shown here to a local market or "hot bazaar" often set up at a "chowtra" or rest stop along the trail.

Foreword

The pictures in this volume were taken from 1972 to 1974 while I served as a Peace Corps volunteer, teaching math and science in a small village in central Nepal called Damaulie. They span the time from my first days of language training in Kathmandu, the capital of Nepal, until my return to the United States. The bulk of the text consists of extracts from letters written at that time and sent to family members back home in Michigan. However, in order to fit into the present narrative, some of the dates of these letters have been altered.

Over the years many changes have occurred. The political system in Nepal has radically altered and the monarchy and monarchs mentioned in my letters are long gone. The events and scenes captured 36 years ago record life in a by-gone era. Technological advances have improved many of the labor intensive activities of villagers in Nepal and around the world. Electricity for one, and improved transportation for another, have enabled many modern conveniences to reach even rural areas of countries such as Nepal. Recently I received a photo of the current school building in Damaulie, sent via e-mail. The photo as well as it's method of delivery show the vast improvement in infrastructure and communications that have taken place since my days there.

The passage of years likewise has brought remarkable advances in printing technology, digital rendering and the internet, and have made publication of this volume possible. An early draft of this volume was pieced together in 1976 using a typewriter and photographic prints. In order to prepare the present volume, the photos which languished as transparencies, prints or negatives have been salvaged and digitally retouched. A badly discolored yet remarkable student's letter I managed to save from destruction 38 years ago has also been restored and preserved in digital form. More recently, correspondence via e-mail with individuals from my Peace Corps days have sparked a desire to create this volume as a testament to the lives and struggles of the marvelous individuals depicted herein. It is to their memory and honor that this book is dedicated.

Midland, Michigan June 2012

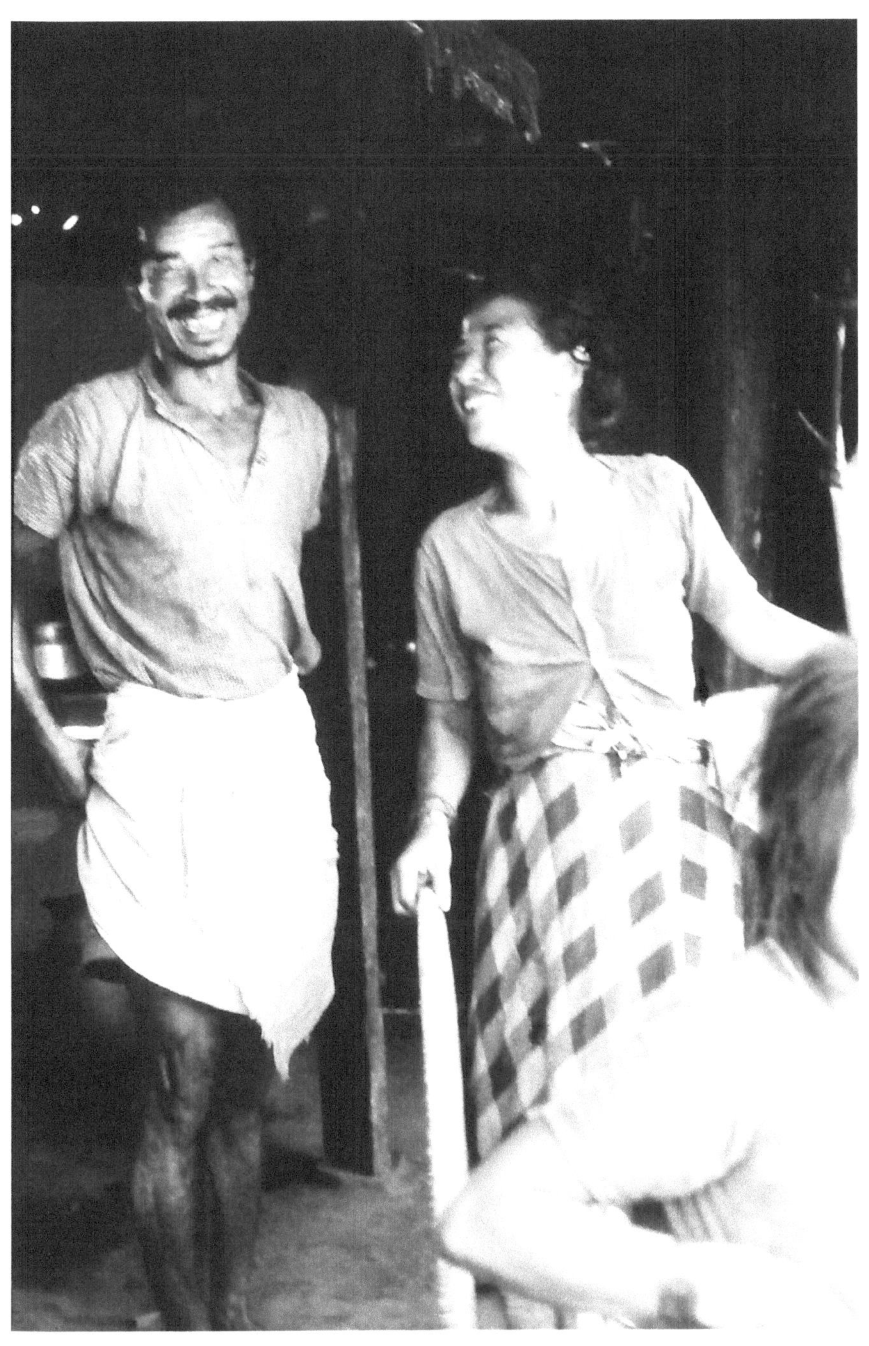

my cook, confidant and tutelary, Didi and her husband, Daju. The words mean elder sister and elder brother but are used to address any older woman or man.

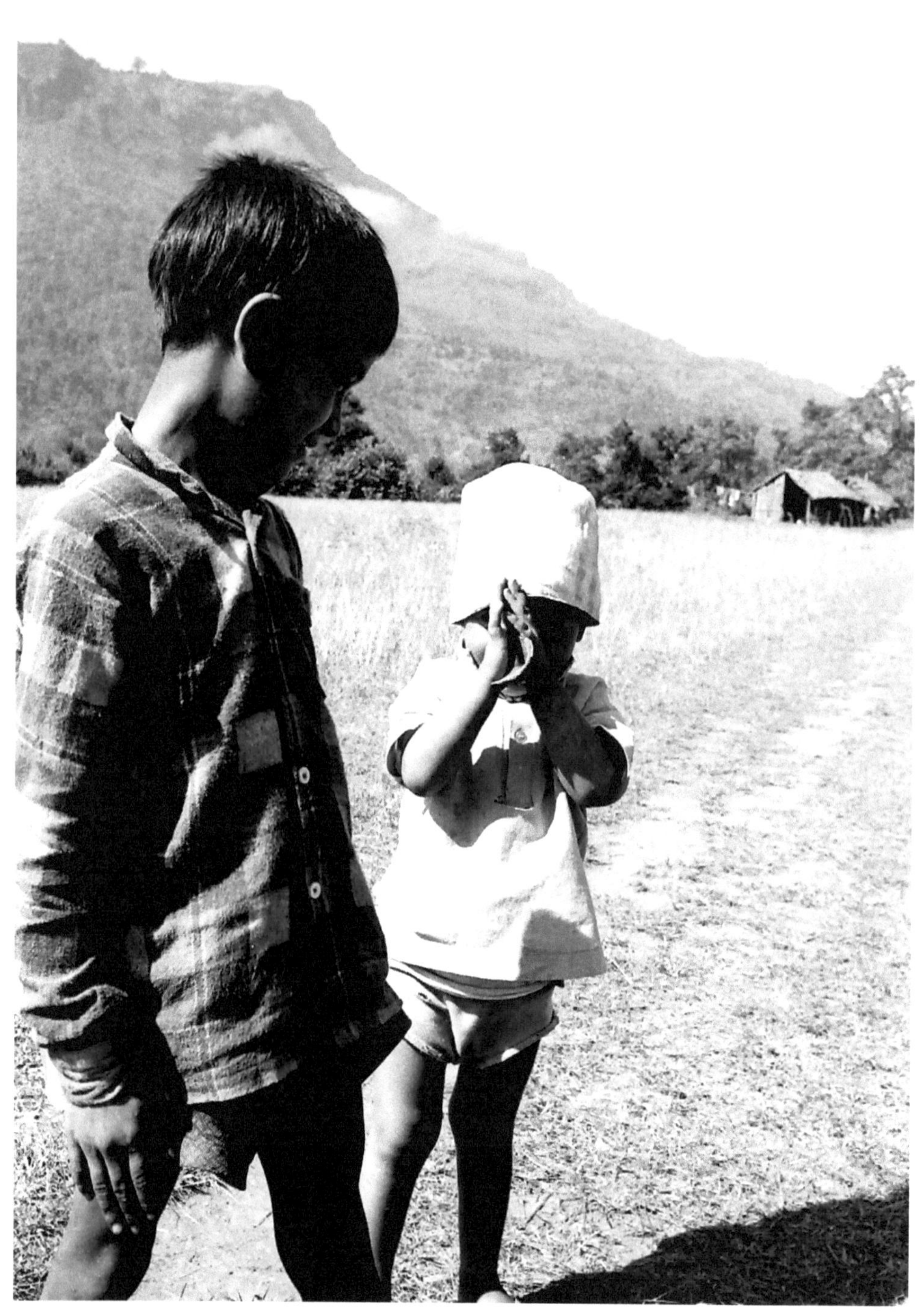

Nameste, the universal greeting

Pokhara, September 4, 1972

Dear Ones All,

Language training is being conducted in this small city west from Kathmandu and about in the center of the country. We will be here three weeks. The routine is six hours of language instruction followed by some special project; like go to the bazaar, (the part of the village where the shops are located) and buy some fruit. That gets us out with the people to use our language.

Today our four day rain let up and Mark, another volunteer, and I went shopping for some kera (bananas). I paid one rupee for five and thought that was fair enough (1 rupee equals ten cents). Mark wanted to try his hand at bargaining though. After ten minutes of frantic arm waiving, pointing and some bargaining he returned from the far end of the bazaar with eight for one and a half rupees. I wonder who learned more, the farmer or Mark?

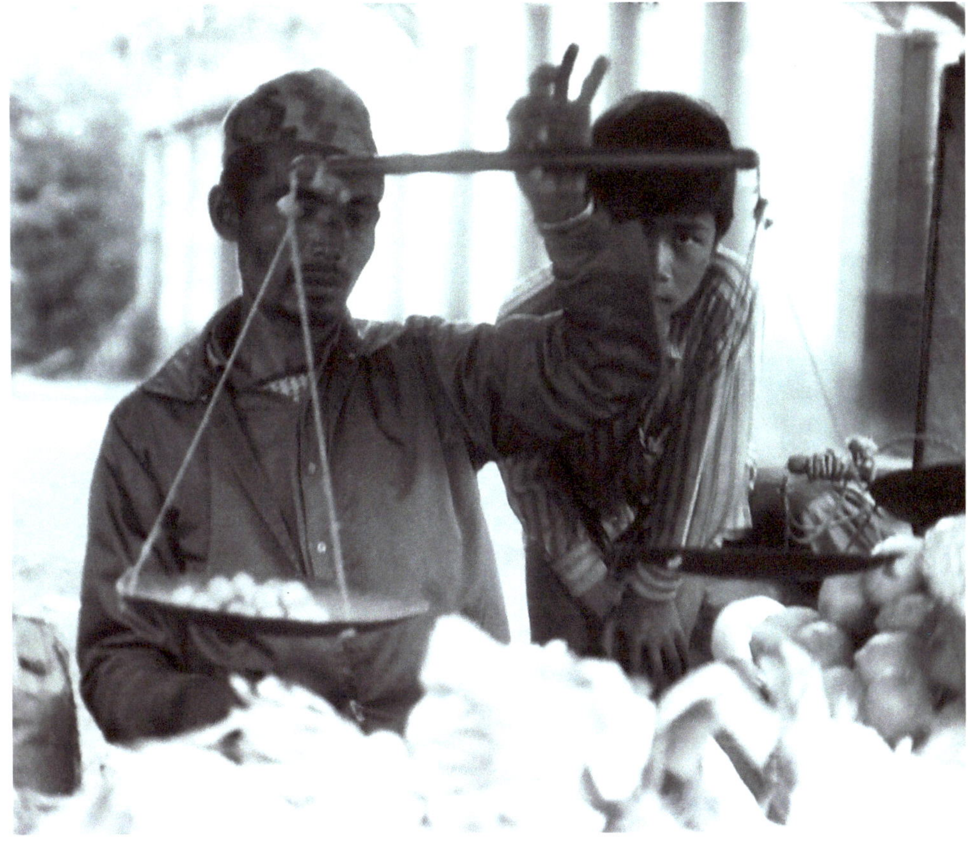

Checking the weight

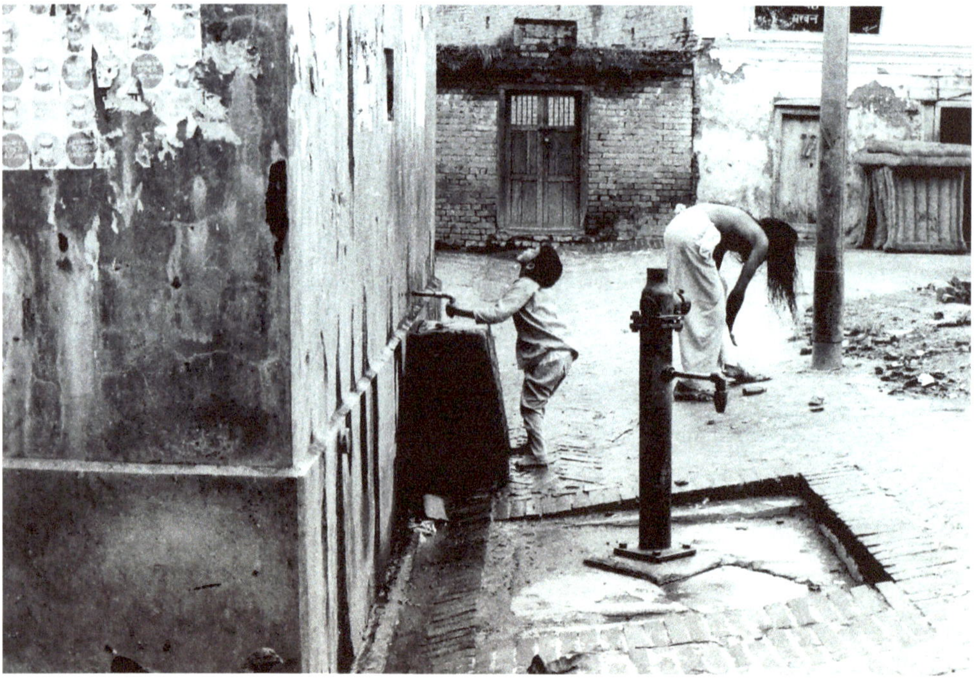

morning scene

Kathmandu

Busy and cosmopolitan with some of the trappings of a modern city, Kathmandu is the capital of Nepal. Most volunteers found it loud, dirty and nauseating, but sufferable if one desired a hot shower and western food. Peace Corps headquarters were located here, making occasional visits to the city a necessity. Initial language training and cultural acclimation took place here.

frozen treat

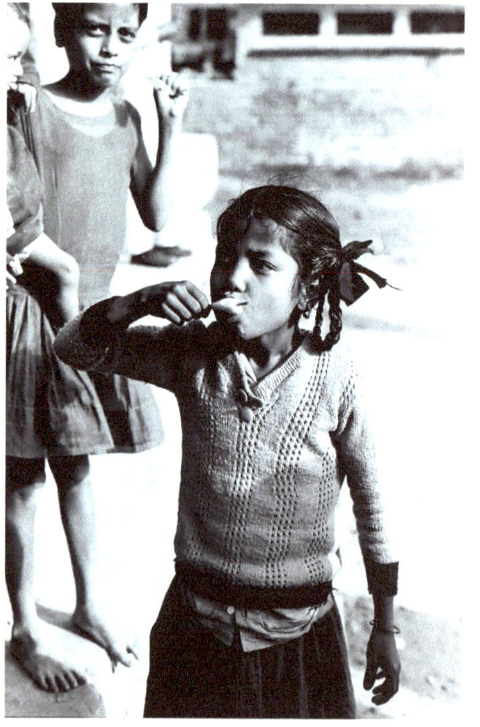

at the Mandir- a Buddhist temple made from a large mound of dirt covered with cement. Notice the kite remains wrapped around the electrical wires. Especially during the fall and winter months kites would be flown from the streets and the flat roofs of buildings. Neighbors competed to see who could cut the other participants' kite strings.

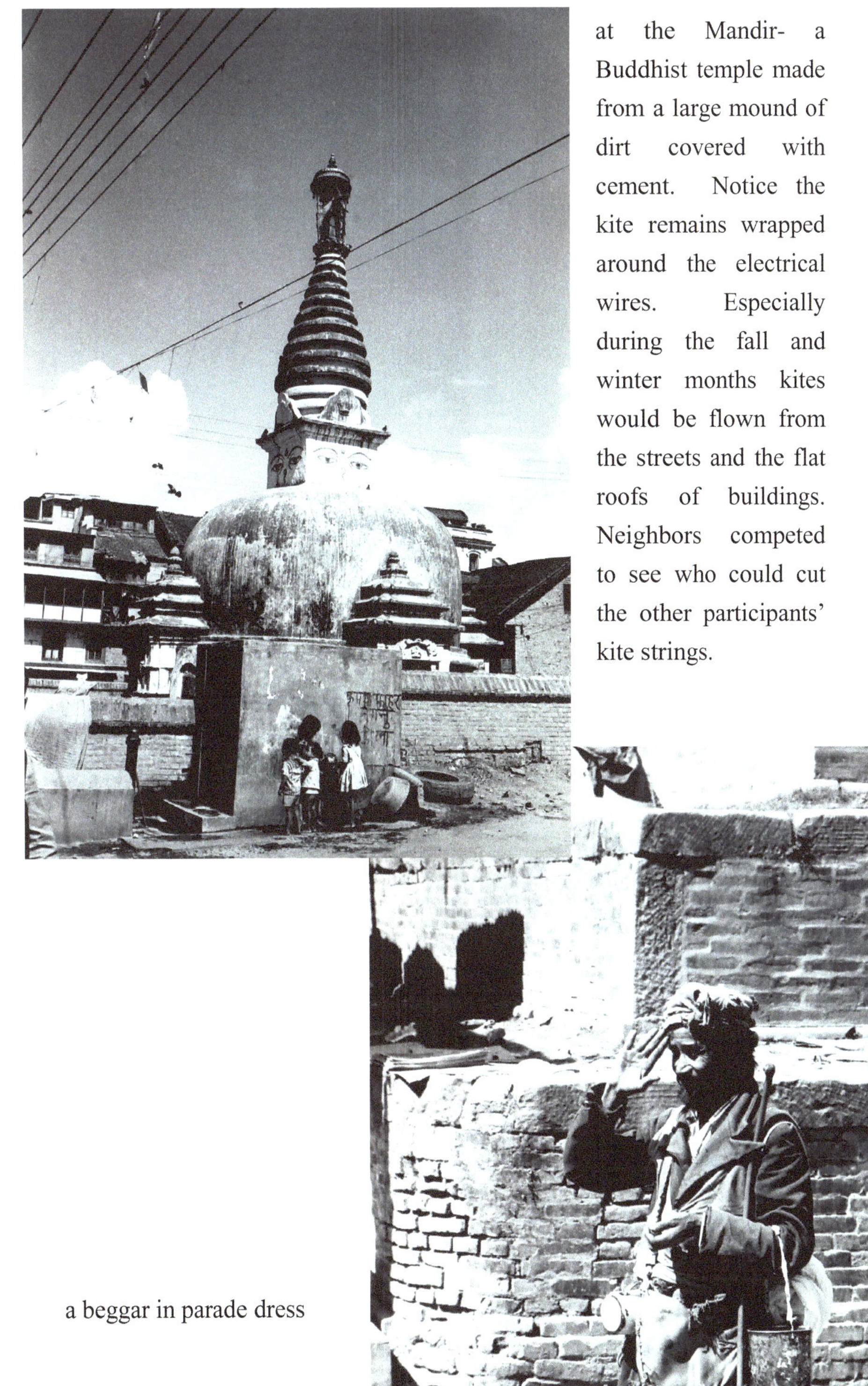

a beggar in parade dress

Damaulie, October 16, 1972

I really know what subsistence farming is about now. I've been staying with Bim Bahadur Chetry while practice teaching these few weeks in Damaulie. He owns two or three acres of land and supports a wife and four children, a mother-in-law, and a hired hand. During the rainy season beginning in June he plants rice. This is harvested in October. Next, wheat is planted and later one of several fast growing plants: mustard for oil, peanuts or dahl (lentils eaten cooked with rice), or corn.

He keeps one half of his rice and some of the corn. The rest is sold. The waste land: pathways, ditch banks, are used for growing greens for his two bissee (water buffalo).

Each morning things start quite early. Everything is done with regularity. About six o'clock I hear the first stirrings. Bim and his family sleep upstairs, while Babu, the hired hand, and I sleep downstairs. Bim calls downstairs the first thing, "Babu, Babu, utta."

It is chilly mornings and it takes two or three times before Babu rolls around. Soon the whole house is stirring. Babu shuffles in bare feet across the bare ground before the house and out to the fields to cut grass for the bissee. Wife silently descends and goes across the yard to the cooking house. Soon smoke pours from the door and windows and tea is ready.

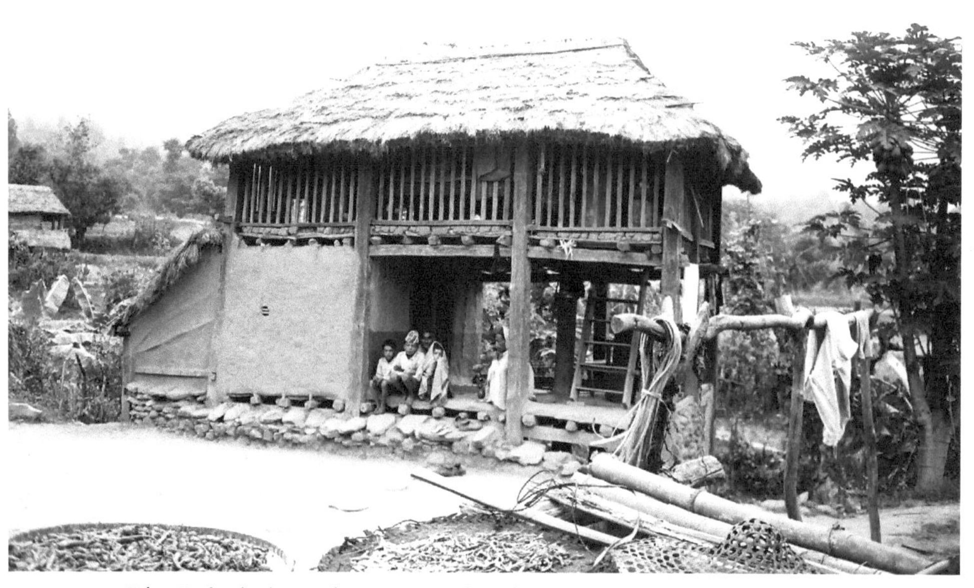

Bim Bahadur's modest yet comfortable house. Babu is seated on the right.

The kids troop down pulling on their shorts and go to work. First a trip to the far side of the yard to the bathroom. Then fires are started to cook mash for the bissee. Branches are brought for the goats. The chickens are the special concern of the little girl; a cutie if ever there was one. Each morning she loads the old hen into a small wicker basket upstairs where they are kept for the night to protect them from rats or other dangers. The hen clucks concernedly until a few of her chicks are added. Finally all the chicks are captured and the hen sits nonchalantly surveying all, content to chirp occasionally to let all know she's ready to be taken downstairs for another day. The girl picks up the small basket, calling for a few additional clucks, and places it inside a larger one. This she places on her back held in place by a trump line across her forehead. The stairs are notches cut in a narrow post set nearly vertical. She backs downstairs with her charge clucking and peeping routinely even when the basket slips a bit in the sling, and sets them free in the yard.

The women begin their day's work. Wife (I never learned her name, only her husband is supposed to hear that) grinds corn with a mill that is no different from one used a thousand years ago. A stone with a hole in the center is turned upon a flat stationary bottom stone. The grain is added in the hole and crushed between the two stones, falling to the mud floor. The ground corn is swept up, boiled and eaten in place of rice.

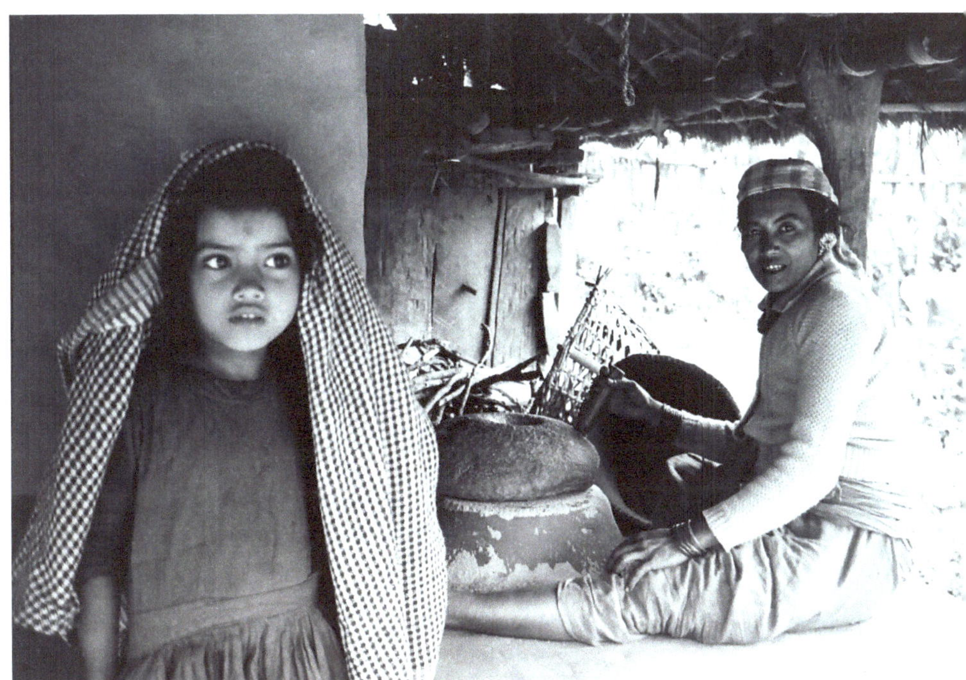

A cutie if ever there was one

Meanwhile, Mother-in-law works a heavy wooden rice mill. She steps on to one end of a beam lifting it into the air and then lets it fall onto a pile of rice. This knocks the outer husk from the rice. Then she winnows it by shaking it in a shallow woven tray. Husks go in one pile to be boiled for the bissee, the clean rice into another for morning "bhat" or boiled rice. Years of experience make a master rice polisher.

Caca, or mother-in-law

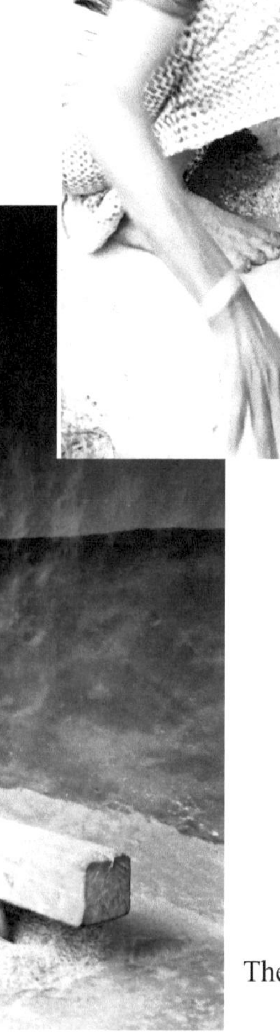

The rice polisher

What makes today different from every other day? Today the King will come to Pokhara! All those who are faithful subjects must journey to Pokhara to see the King and Queen. All buses, trucks, and cars traveling to Pokhara must give free transportation to those walking. Last night other important officials in the local government whose houses were farther away, stayed overnight with Bim. Early in the morning, wife was up. Bhat had to be prepared early today! Last evening a double supply of grass and leaves was brought in for the bissee. The children were all told to obey Caca, who was too old to make the trip.

Bhat is ready now and the men eat quickly. Hurry now, it's a long trip ahead. There would be nothing more to eat until long after dark this day. Afterwards, they select their best coat, clean it carefully with their hands and wipe out the wrinkles. Each has a tiny name tag. Can you read my name? Do you think he will even see me? Each adjusts his cap a hundred times. Finally, all are ready. Fastening on their only pair of sandals, reserved for special occasions, they trek off to the bazaar.

Meanwhile, Wife hurriedly eats her bhat. She wouldn't allow herself to eat with the men. Then she rinses the flat brass plates, places them away, and runs upstairs. This is the big day. Long ago she had decided just how to braid her hair. Carefully she selects her one new blouse. It stands out against the faded and worn sari. Oh, what it had meant to buy the material for that blouse. She had sat in the cloth shop for hours just looking at all the colors before deciding. How she wished she could have a new blouse for each day!

Downstairs again. She must hurry to catch the men. She stops, her heart pounding with excitement, her scalp tingling from the vigorous combing. A word to the children and off she runs, barefoot to the bazaar and the bus stop. Her oiled black braids sail behind her. How happy she is that her husband allowed her to go! What do you suppose the Queen will wear? Does she have new blouses every day?

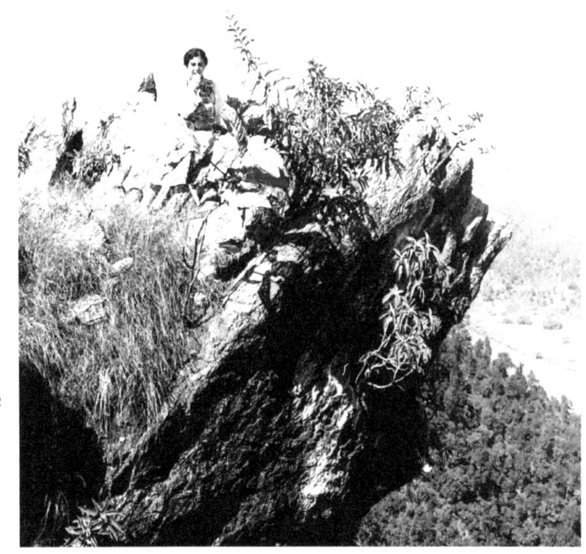

The small hills around Damaulie are mountains in their own right.

Damaulie, December 8, 1972

At last, training is over! We've all received our posts and I elected to come to Damaulie after living there for the few weeks of practice teaching and seeing what it had to offer. I've been here two weeks, but won't begin to teach until the new school year starts on January 1. In the meantime, there's lots of work. I've finished my outdoor john. The salient features of this model are the solid mahogany floor and thatch roof. I've told everyone that they are welcome to use it too. I see some have, though the little ones sometimes forget to lift the trap door in the floor first.

The next problem will be the rats. At night it sounds like a free for all in my room. I've also planted a small garden. Lettuce and radishes are up already. They should taste good in a few weeks.

I also hope to take a short hike towards the mountains before school begins.

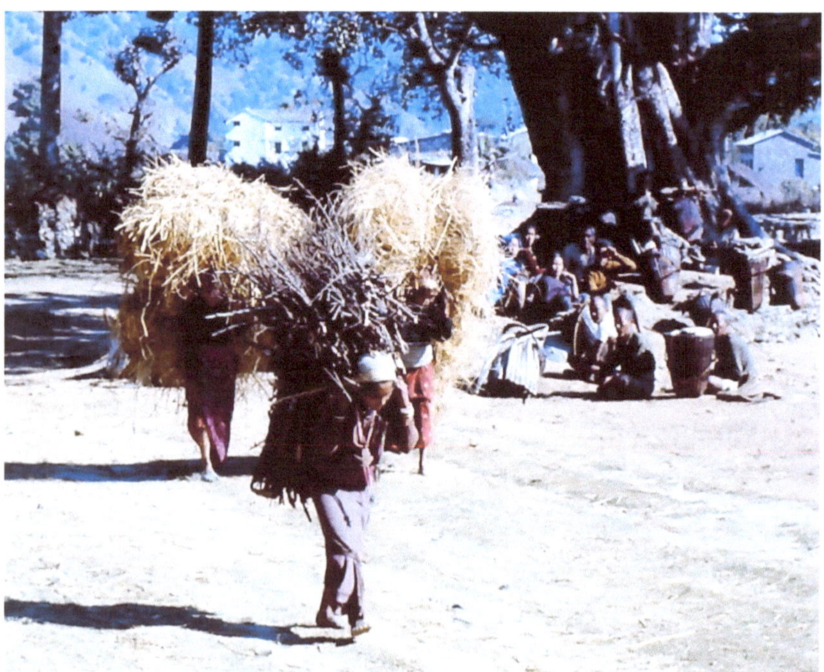

A "chowtra" or rest stop along the trail with giant "peeple" (banyon) trees. Women are free in this workers' paradise to carry as much as any man. Most existing villages are located at the tops of hills to avoid the malaria invested valleys. Everything of commerce moves between them on the backs of porters. The new paved road from Kathmandu west mostly follows river valleys, and is causing new villages to spring up along its route.

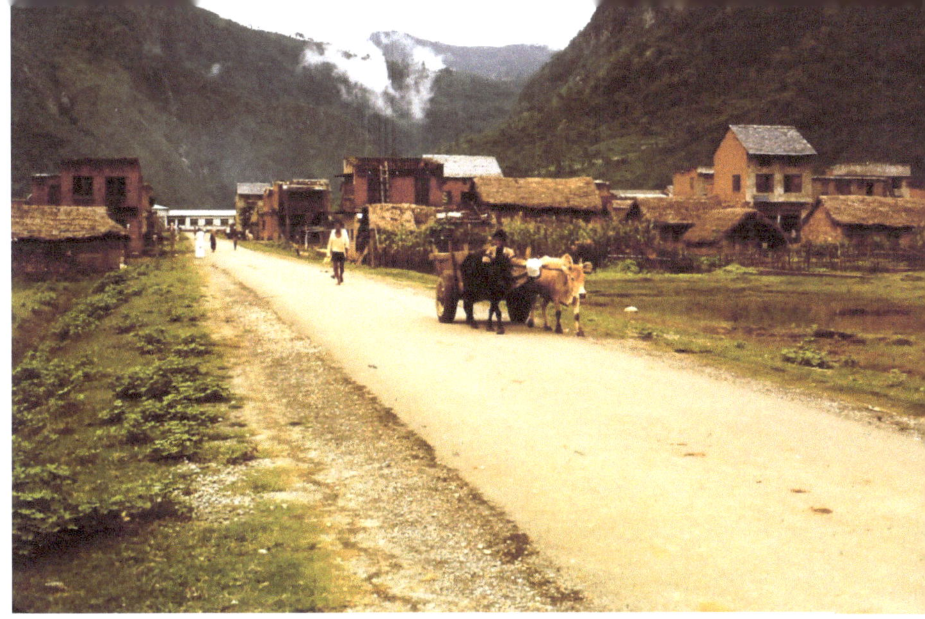

Damaulie Bazaar - During my stay, a group of Chinese engineers in charge of building a highway from Kathmandu to Pokhara were also located in the area. The local officials convinced them to include the entrance to Damaulie in the scope of work. The actual workers were all local Nepalese, mostly women, who used hammers all day to bust large rocks into gravel to make the asphalt paving.

Damaulie, December 22, 1972

Dear All,

Things don't start happening around here until after morning bhat. It's usually chilly so everyone stands around until then, wrapped in a blanket and sipping tea. I'll attempt to use the time to write a letter describing my first few days here and my room.

Damaulie is a dusty, five hour bus ride west from Kathmandu. I stayed the first few nights in a ramshackle "bhutee" (inn) near the bus stop. When I met the headmaster of my high school we began looking around for a better place to stay. Nothing was available in the bazaar, which was just fine, since things there are just so busy, it would be hard to find privacy. So, we went to a little village about one mile east of Damaulie, but closer to the high school. Here there were two small stores, two tea "pausals" and several small mud huts. One of the stores had a small room on the first floor available and I latched on to it.

It's about fifteen feet square and came with a plank bed and a mud floor! But, the price was right, three dollars a month. Well, I carried my stuff over from the bhutee and began to remodel a little. A doorway had been left between my room and the shop owner's cooking room next door. Twice a day the rats and I were driven out by the clouds of smoke that filled the room and overflowed out the windows.

I now know why Nepalese always squat instead of stand or sit on furniture. The top half of the room is always filled with smoke! Locally made bricks are available. So I bought some and set about sealing off the unwanted chimney. As long as I was at it, I included a built-in writing table, ending up with a real nice partition. The bricks aren't fired hard enough to fuse the clay, and since I was only using wet clay for mortar, I suppose the rats will be able to tunnel through my new wall just like the rest of the walls.

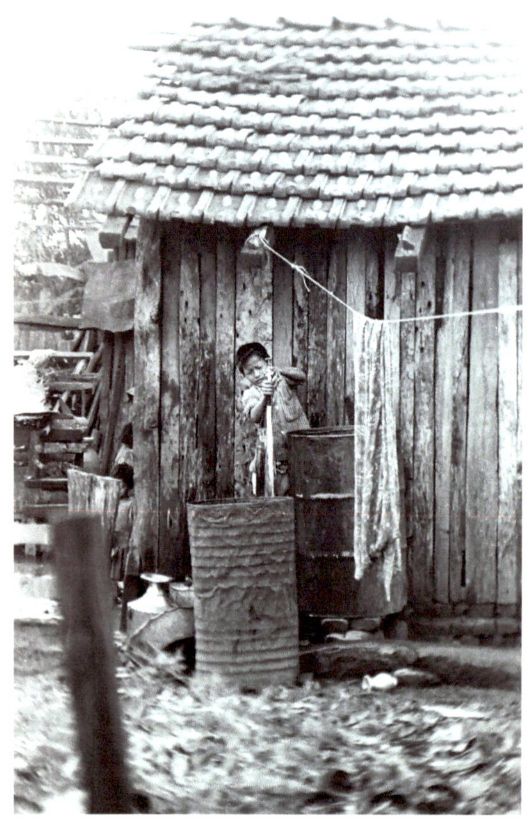

The bazaar had clean water at several spigots. I paid Didi to carry a clay pot of water up the hill to my room each day. An iodine pill in each pot insured safe drinking water.

Because of the dirt "bartho's" or pathways, you constantly have to wash your feet. Flip-flops are the footwear of choice for those who can afford them. There were several streams in the area which provided convenient bathing sites. Women bathed mostly in the morning when frequent fogs provided more discrete bathing conditions.

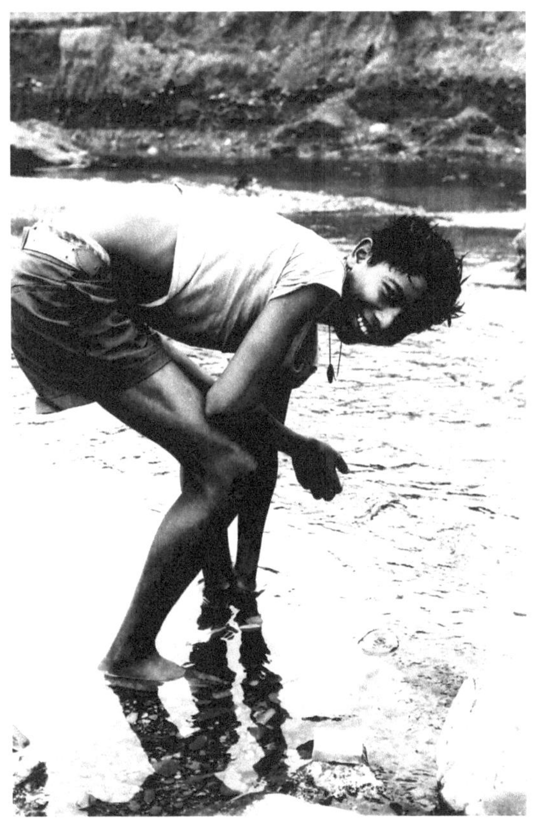

Damaulie, January 3, 1973

The basic color scheme in most Nepalese homes is dirt brown mixed with smoke. However, the tea shop next door where I've been eating has white washed walls. I asked the Didi running the shop who had done her walls. She said that she had and that she would do my walls also. She cooked rice flour into a paste an added gray clay from the river. So today and yesterday we've been plastering. It lightens the room well and sticks to the wall without rubbing off. If she could make something in a high gloss I'd let her do the woodwork also.

After Didi finished plastering, she informed me my floors needed remudding, and she was just the one to do it. Before I had time to disagree, she carried a pile of wet clay and cow manure to my door and dumped it on my floor. Then she told me to start mixing while she added more water. So, when your Didi tells you to do something you hop right to it. We soon had a fresh coat of mud on the floor. I still don't know what the manure adds. Perhaps it keeps the clay moist. It doesn't seem to smell, or maybe I've just gotten used to the odor by now.

That about finishes the redecorating. I bought a few rice straw mats for the floor and for use as a mattress for my bed. As a final touch, I built a little oven in one corner of the room out of a biscuit tin and some left over bricks. I see now my baked Alaska is about done, so I had better close.

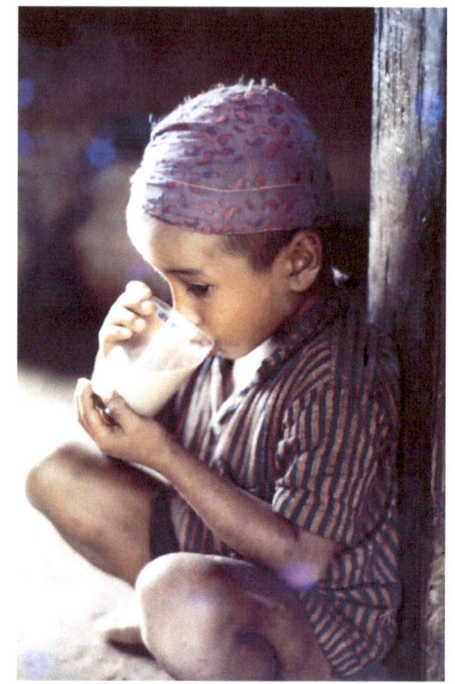

sipping tea

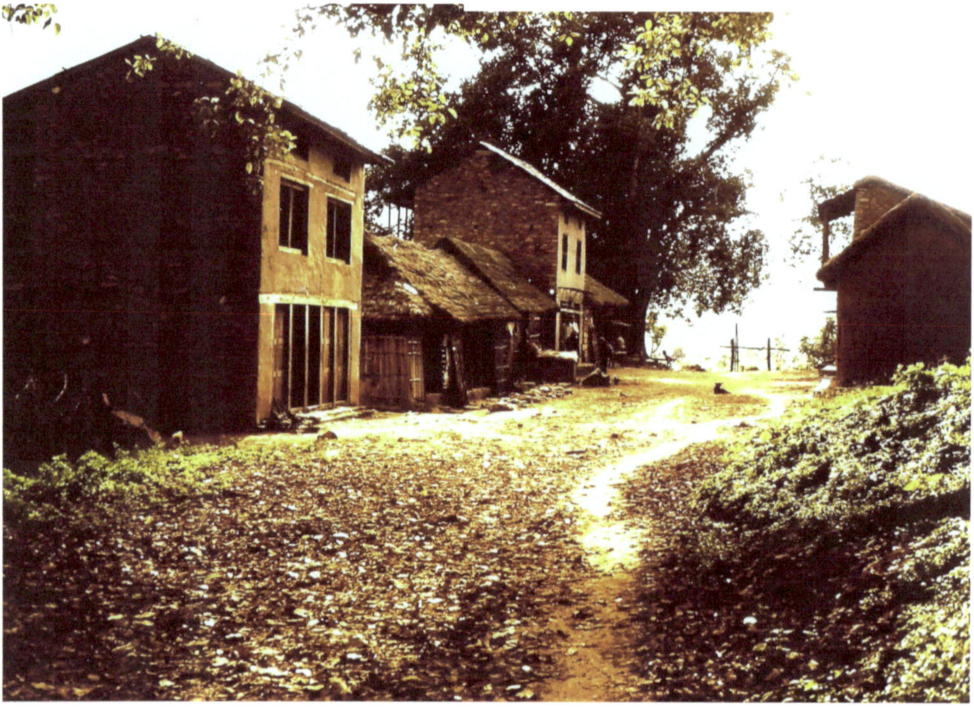

home- My room was on the back side of the first house on the left

Damaulie, January 10, 1073

A few evenings ago I settled down after evening bhat and soon began to feel drowsy. We eat after dark. Didi and her family work long and hard while there is light. But now the sound of drums from other distant huts floated into my room; a gentle boom-gung, boom-gung… I could imagine the faces beside a fire, laughing, glittering, singing. It was a happy evening at the close of a hard day, and I slumbered off.

Soon afterward I was jolted awake by Didi's terrified screaming and pounding at my door. I couldn't understand what was happening, but jumped from bed, pulled on my shorts and flung the bar from the door. She rushed in, grabbed my water pot, and like a flash, fled again. I stood in my doorway and finally understood what had happened. The last house along the row of huts, a tea pasaul, was on fire! A dull orange glow illuminated the other stick and thatch huts of the village. Sparks rose into the warm night air. If one landed on a neighbor's roof, it too could go up in flames until the whole village was destroyed. I quickly grabbed my plastic pail and ran to the scene.

Everywhere men were calling for more water and feverishly pulling at the thatch and burning sticks of the roof in an effort to stop the flames. Water was urgently needed. Several people ran to the stream hundreds of yards distant carrying brass and clay pots. At first I pulled off my shirt and attempted to beat the flames. But the fire burned too swiftly and was on the underside of the tinder dry roofing so my beating had little effect. Nearly a quarter of the roof was destroyed already. One wall was made of woven twigs and grass. This was hurriedly torn down and the tea pasaul owner's meager possessions dragged into the middle of the dirt street.

By now, water had begun to arrive, and I began to use my bucket to good advantage on the furiously burning roof. The local water pots could not be used to throw water because of their narrow tops designed to keep the water from spilling while being carried. Before I arrived, hands had been about the most effective weapon against the flames. Also, I quickly found the water had to be thrown from inside the hut because the natural construction of the thatch shed any water thrown from above.

After perhaps fifteen minutes of intense work the flames were quelled. Afterwards, we walked among the debris, carefully rubbing water on even the minutest live ember until all were extinguished. The women's sobs and smelly smoke and steam still coming from the ruined hut were all that remained to remind us of one family's loss, and the village's close brush with tragedy.

I withdrew from the scene. Already those present were relating their particular efforts and thoughts on the evening's events, while others joined in and commented in noisy order. Returning to my apartment, I picked up my kerosene stove. Luckily, some milk from afternoon remained for tea. The water was soon hot and the tea gladly accepted by those left homeless in the middle of the night.

Next morning the sun rose warm and cherry orange above the mist covered hills. The rice mill in the bazaar began it's loud staccato, "thaat, thaat, thaat," signaling the start of another day's work. Farmers called to their oxen across the fields. Just like yesterday, or a thousand years ago, the tips of small wooden plows dug once again into the deep red earth.

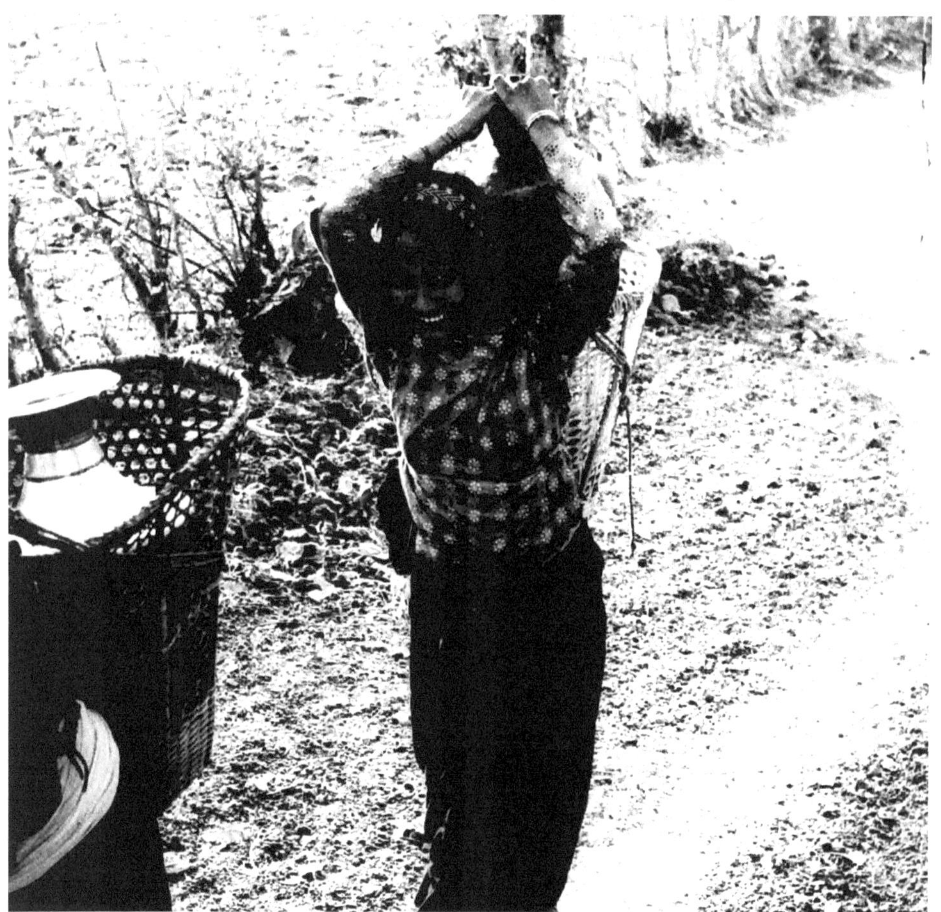

Nepalese water pots make poor fire buckets. The nearest water source was a small spring, one half mile away.

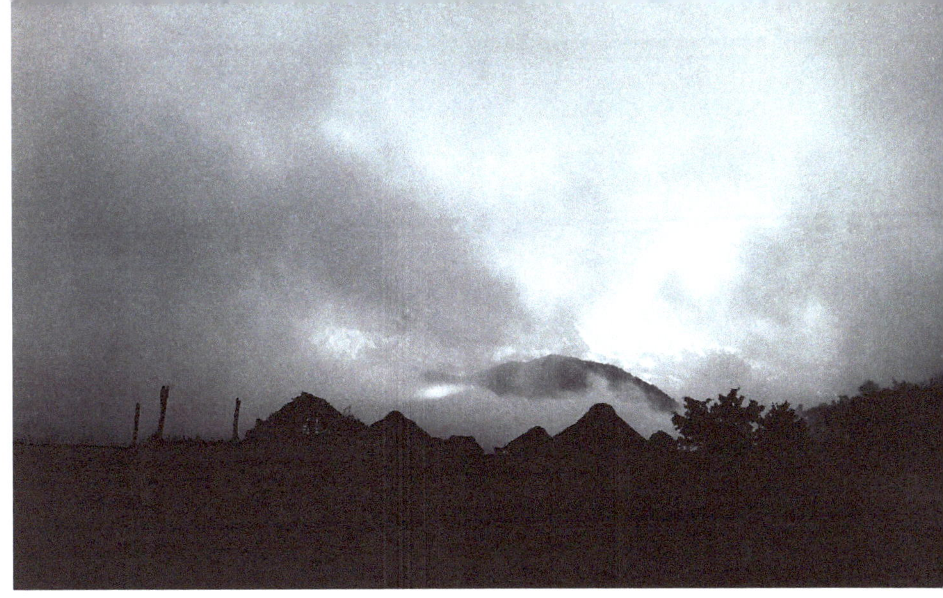

morning mist with Himalayas in distance

Damaulie, January 17, 1973

The garden has met with disaster. A local herd of goats took just one pass to clean me out. But I have a friend in similar straits. The contractor working on our new high school building had a hundred tangerine seedlings growing in a shady spot. He thought they were protected from all known digging, browsing or otherwise destructive pests. But his own chickens proved his downfall, as one afternoon, six months of hopeful expectation ended in one flurry of scratching.

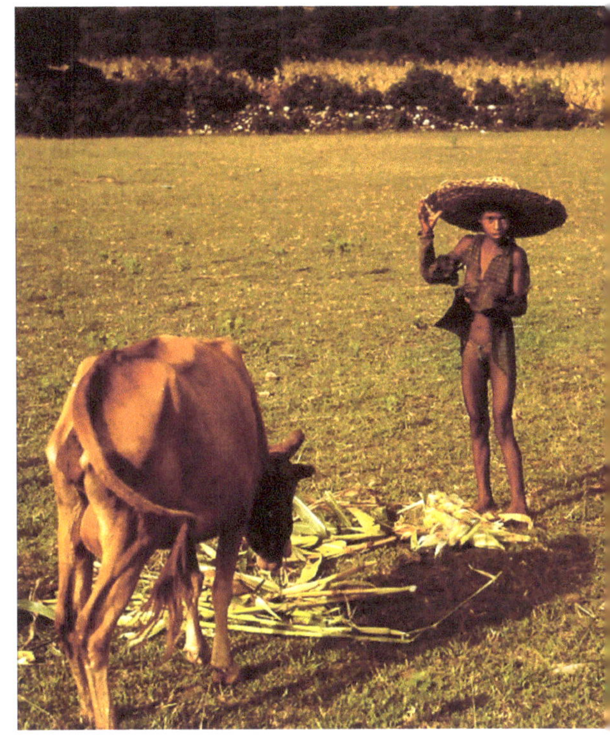

a prime suspect

Damaulie, January 26, 1973

We've had some interesting folk dancing the past week. The evenings have been long and cool and a few hours together singing and dancing are the rewards for a hard day laboring in the corn fields. I received a special invitation, so last night, I too joined in the festivities. The men (including yours truly) sat on the ground before a villager's small hut with our instruments: wooden drums covered with stretched lizard or goat skin. The leader chanted his favorite lyrics while we aspiring drummers provided nearly the same beat over and over again. Those who knew the words joined in and the song built to a peak of excitement; then quickly ended in a few sharp slaps on the drums.

The women dancers were the unmarried girls from our village. All had dressed in the finest saris, jewels and bangles they could find, and wove to and fro, moving their arms in unison, stamping their feet, shaking their bangles to the beat. They presented a very pleasing appearance.

The dance was composed of only a few movements and like the music, not very complex. One dancer occasionally would break from the rest after their denouement was reached, and attempt to touch all the drums before the drummers finished wrapping out a few last beats. This was the ultimate in daring, and brought much coy laughter as she returned to her friends.

So on it went, everyone laughing and enjoying the scene, especially when the new drummer was too slow to catch a change in rhythm. Oh, I suppose if I had kept at it I would have gotten as good as the next guy. But, when it was quite late, I decided to call it quits. So, I excused myself from the happy crowd, melted away from the circle of faces lit by the kerosene lantern and came back to my own room.

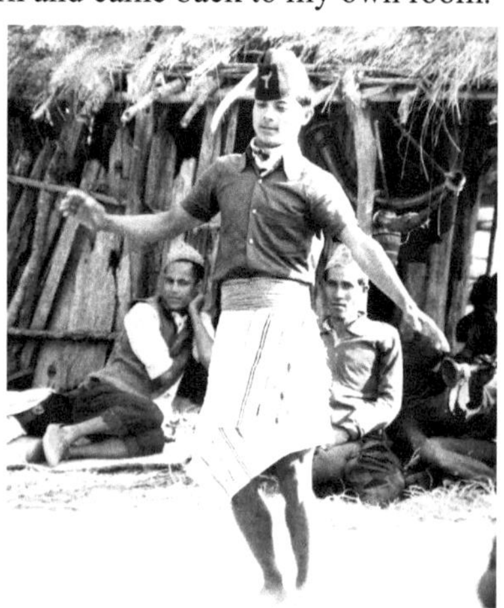

dancing

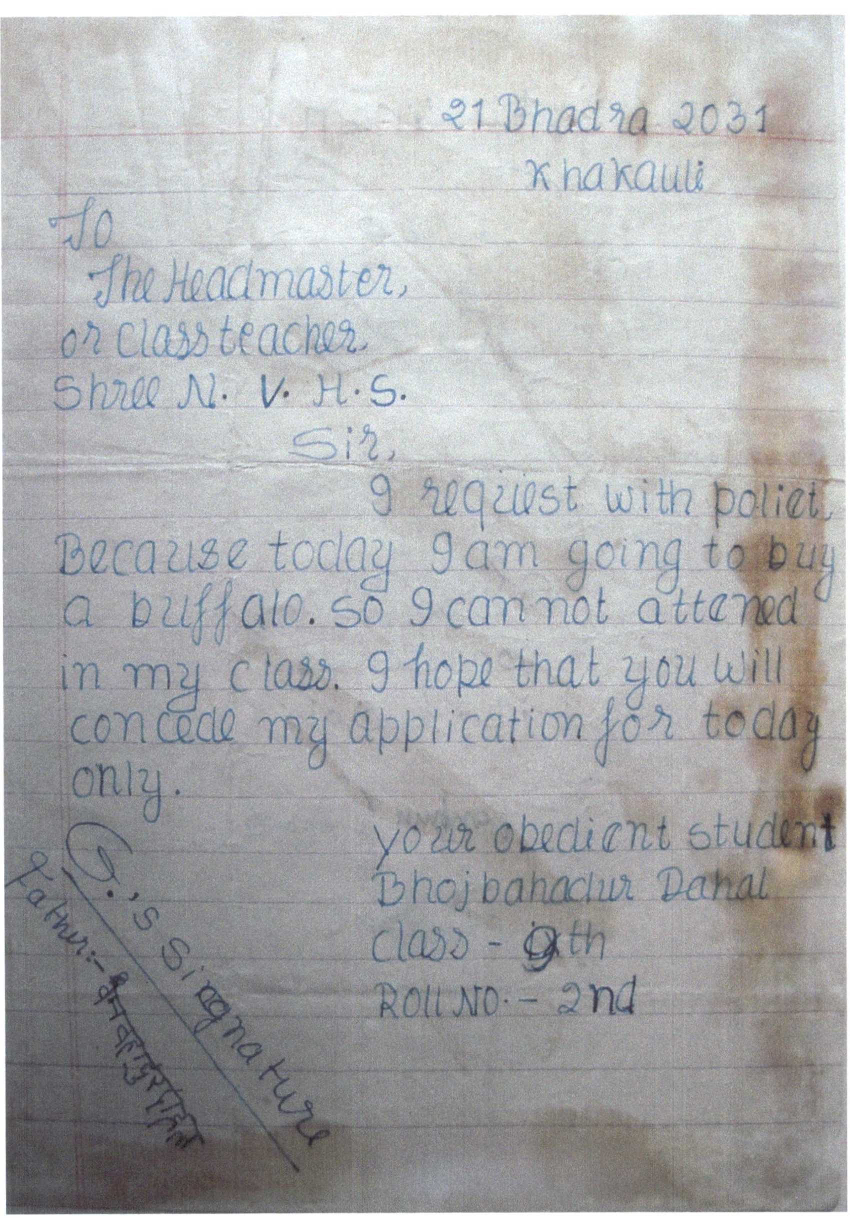

21 Bhadra 2031
Khakauli

To
The Headmaster,
or Class teacher
Shree N. V. H. S.

Sir,
I request with polite. Because today I am going to buy a buffalo. so I can not attened in my class. I hope that you will concede my application for today only.

your obedient student
Bhojbahadur Dahal
Class - 9th
Roll No. - 2nd

G.'s Signature
Father:-

Student request to be excused from class, with signature of parent

The Nepalese calendar is a solar calendar, but is about 57 years ahead of the modern western calendar. Also, the months are about 15 days different from western months. Bhadra is August - September.

Damaulie, February 9, 1973

Yesterday was a holiday to worship Saraswati, the goddess of education. The kids came to school and did a special "pujja" or sacrifice. It was quite charming. The "Guru," our Sanskrit teacher, acted as Master of Ceremonies. First they mixed some special rice, red powder and sacred milk and then dabbed it on their books, the school, teachers, students, and everything else in sight. Next they mumbled some special prayers and burnt an incense candle. Everyone wore a strip of red or white cotton cloth about their neck to signify the power of education.

The rest of the day was a big feast. The teachers had chipped in to buy a small goat. This was butchered and we had curried meat, vegetables (cauliflower and potatoes), and dried rolled rice, called "churia," all served on hand made leaf plates. I was plugged.

Today was clean up day. The students tore down the decorations and carried the banana stalks that had served as a shrine to the river. After one final shout, everything was thrown in.

So much for education. I wish they would put half as much effort into their homework.

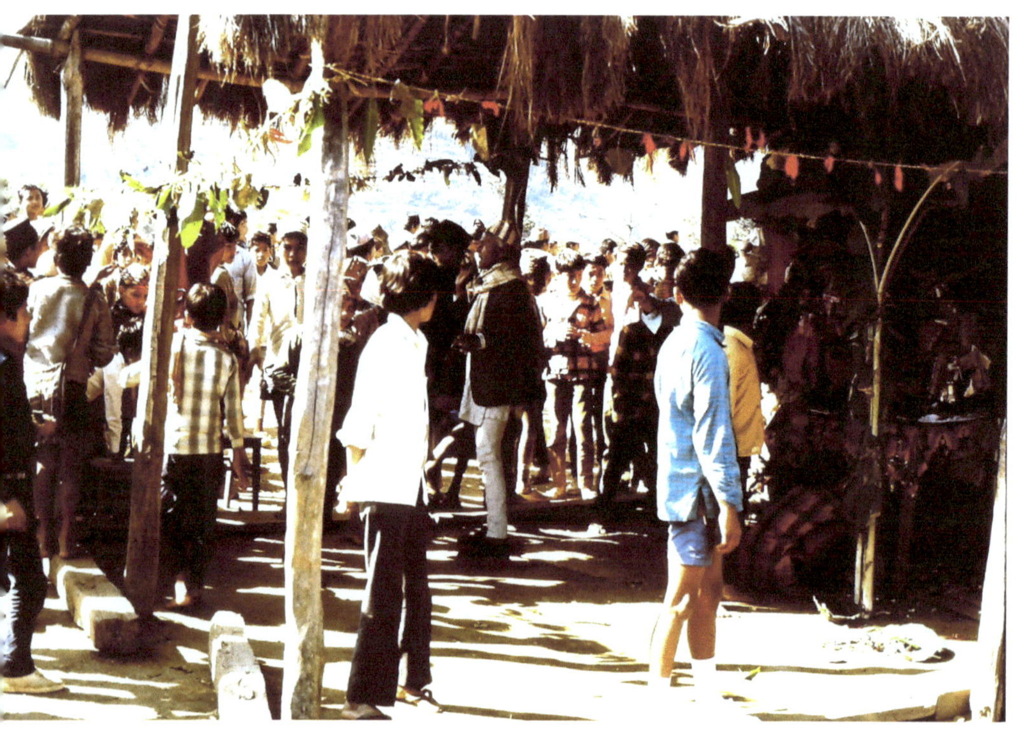

Our Guru led the ceremonies.

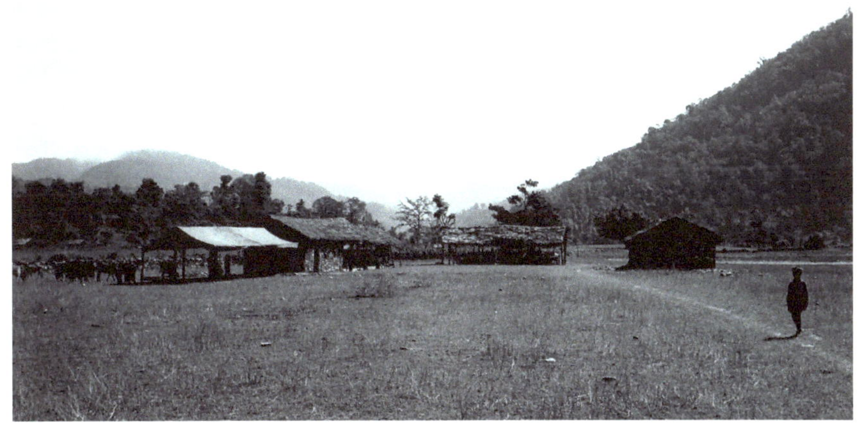

Nirmal High School pre-monsoon

Damaulie, February 22, 1973

There's been an honest to goodness strike by the teachers at school. This place seems to be overrun with pinkoes. They're never satisfied with what they have, but always must be "agitatin" for more. What do you suppose they wanted this time? It wasn't the amount of their wages. Oh, no, that was just fine. It wasn't the cost of living escalator in their contracts, or early retirement, health insurance or any of that other socialist nonsense. No, those weren't the problem at all. Rather, it seems none of the teachers had been paid for over a year.

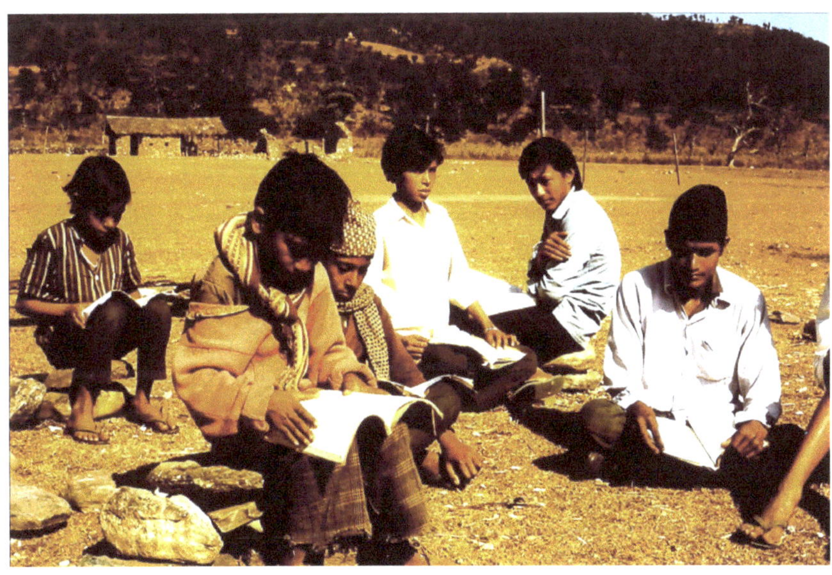

Our high school – or what's left of it

Say, come to think about it, that might set a man a little against the system. But, I wanted to haul the scabs and strike busters in there right away. We've got to stop this creeping socialism somewhere. Next thing you know, they'll be wanting to be paid every Friday.

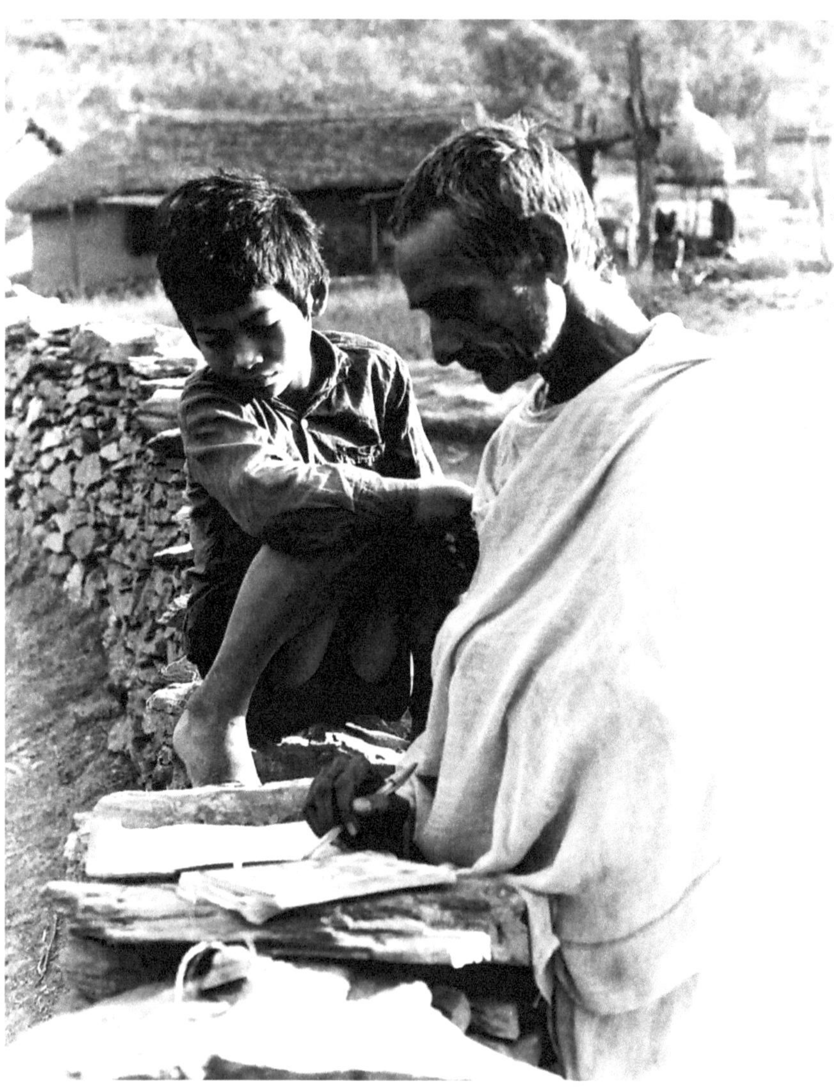

Nepalese can read nearly as easily if the book is upside down as right-side up. This occurs because there are so few books or letters that when one does appear, all crowd around to read it. Youngsters of course end up with the least advantage and spend most of their young lives learning to read form the wrong end of the book.

Damauli, April 6, 1973

I brought a soccer ball from Kathmandu last January for the high school. Due to a rugged bunch of soccer players, a cheap Indian soccer ball and perhaps over inflation on my part, it only lasted one month. Well, I salvaged the inner bladder and leather covering. Now some of the local tots and I have made wonderful slingshots. The kids bring a forked branch that they've cut and we then cut the rubber strips and tie the leather. Now standard equipment on most every village moppet is a sling shot crammed into the back pocket of their shorts. This is no doubt much to the dismay of the local dogs and chickens, which provide excellent targets.

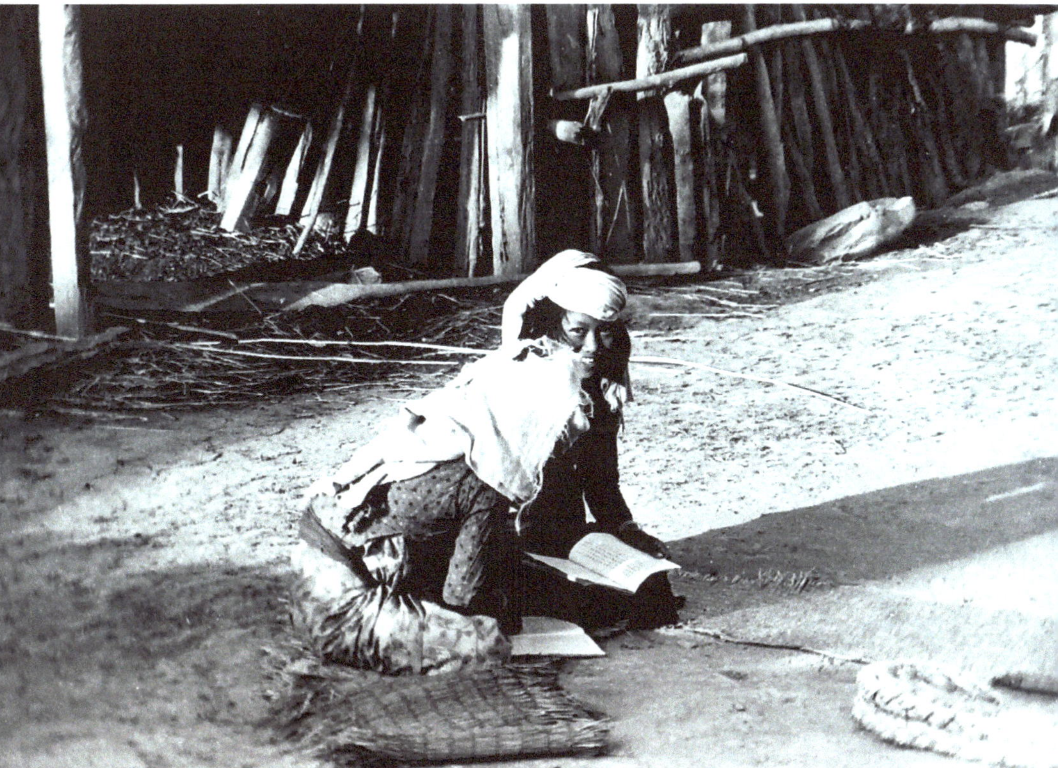

school girls

I began a free school to teach basic reading for children too poor to attend the public school. Class is held in a farmer's yard. That's the pig sty in the background. I pay two local high school students, a boy and girl, to be the teachers. I am the truant officer, chasing down students who have gone "baghio."

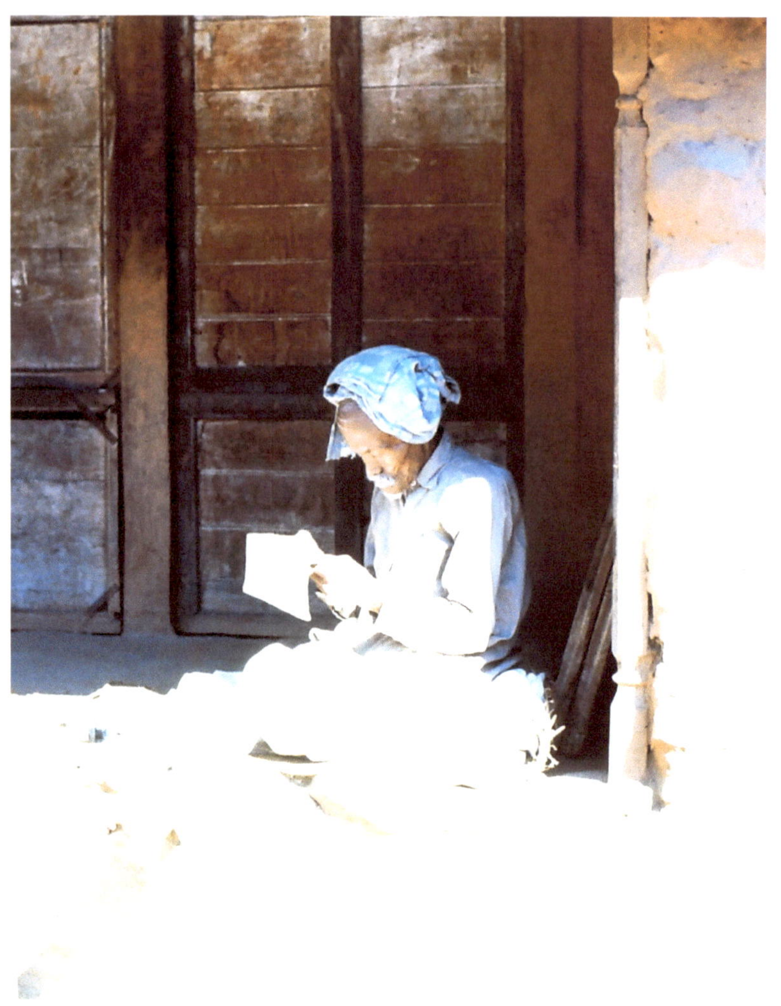

finding the words

Nepalese is the national language. Like Hindi, it is derived from Sanskrit. Literacy, especially in the countryside, is rather low. While I had several months of language training, I found it rather difficult to teach effectively in Nepalese. Fortunately, teaching math could be accomplished with some arm waving and drawing of figures. Science was another story. I used the older students to help create lesson plans and depended a lot on the students reading their textbooks. I got the impression that classes with "Master Sahib" were constant sources of levity.

Damaulie, April 20, 1973

You wanted to know what radio stations I listen to. If I had one good English one I'd be happy. I took the problem to task a while ago and tried to set up a better antenna and ground for my little portable radio. When in Pokhara some time back, I bought some wire and strung forty feet of it around the ceiling of my room. This I wrapped around the tip of the existing antenna. Making a ground was easy. Since my bed is sitting right on good ol' "terra firma," I shoved an old nail into the clay and hitched on the wire. The result was to increase the squeals and howling wonderfully. Also, now I get heavy, revolutionary band music from China.

On that same trip to Pokhara, I brought back some window screening. The flies aren't too thick yet, but with warmer weather coming, I'd better be prepared. However, after tacking it up, I found I had screened in more than I'd screened out. That sets fine with my roommate though. He's a giant spider, five inches across, if he's an inch. Efficient too. Why, doesn't even work with a net. About evening there may be a congregation of twenty or so flies when he slips out from his hiding place in my clean underwear pile. He spends the rest of the night stalking around and jumping several inches to grab dozing flies. He lands on the screen with a great plop, waking me and stirring up a swarm of survivors. Hope he stops growing soon.

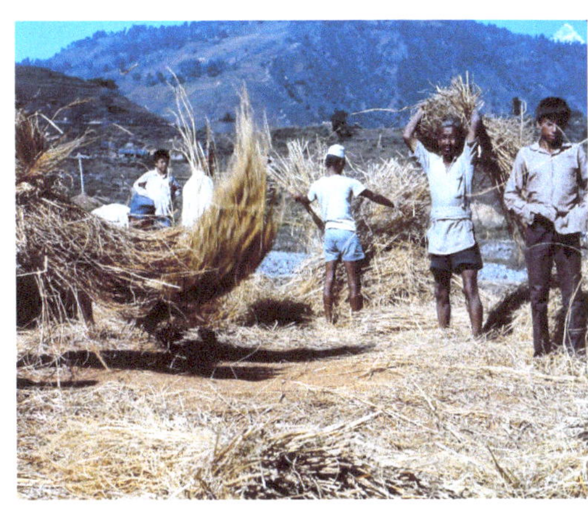

rice harvest

Damaulie, April 27, 1973

A few days ago a tiger raided the village and made off with a little piglet. All the animals nearly went wild from the smell of it. Pigs squealed, the dogs were wound up tight, and scared stiff. This happened at night and before anyone could get out of their huts, pig and tiger both were gone. The ruckus went on for quite some time though. I wonder if it really was a tiger? Maybe it was a little leopard. If I knew it would come back, I would sit up in a tree and maybe catch a view of it. But, then again- what if it was a tiger?

bissee bathing in the ole swimming hole

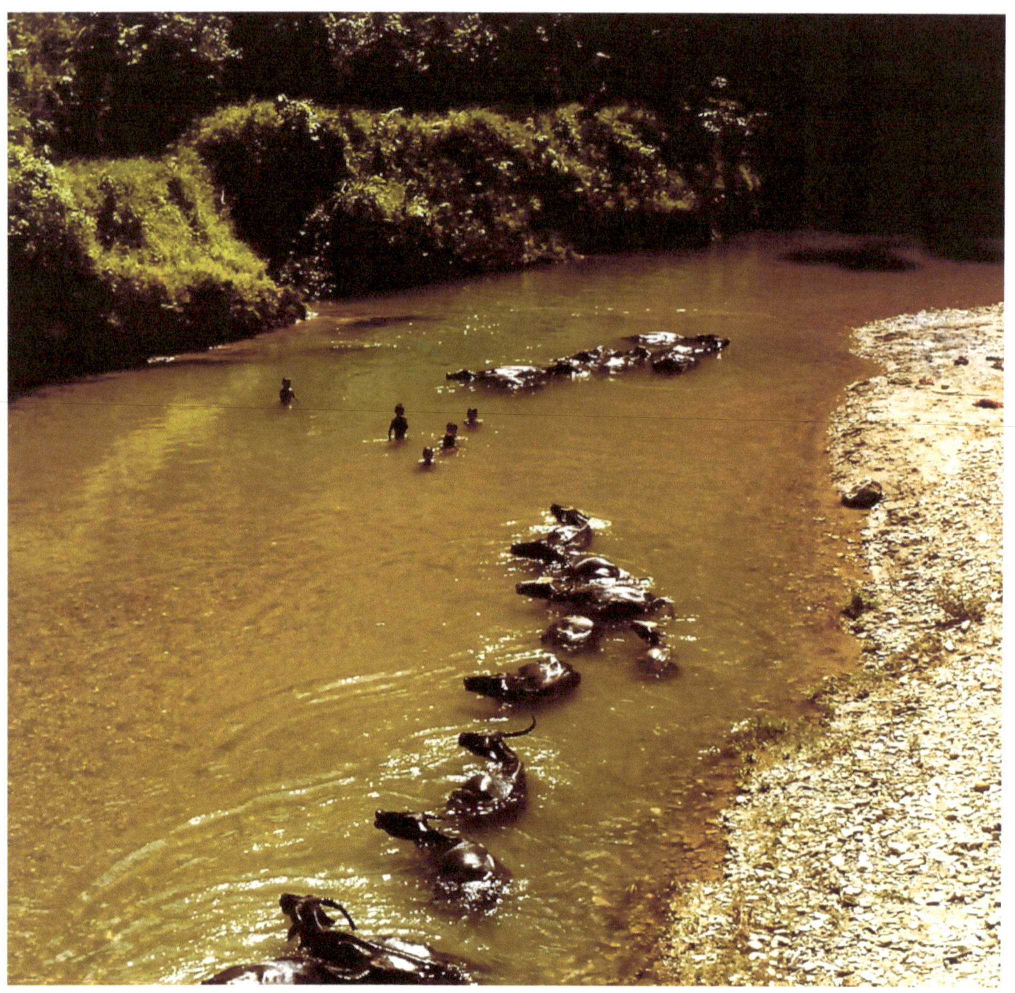

Damaulie, May 7, 1973

This is Buddha's birthday. Every family is doing "pujha" and making special breads for the occasion. It should be quite a nice day.

Despite the holiday, the local hooscow has been filled with unfortunate offenders. They've been clapped behind bars but refuse to quiet down. They stamp their feet and make noise all day long. Each is securely tied to a large post driven into the ground. Some have heavy ropes about their necks, others are tied by the feet. While the inmates aren't able to move around, they can at least keep flies swished off with their tails and they get their daily ration of grass while in "jail." The prison is a village corral for cows, bissee, or goats that sneak away from their masters and raid a neighbor's newly planted corn or rice field. I imagine all the green edibles are mighty tempting after the months of drought.

But everyone must be careful of their animals now, or pay a heavy fine to the victims whose fields are plundered if a cow is locked up for filching corn stalks. I wish I'd gotten a hold of those goats that ruined my garden. But, back then I suppose nothing was supposed to be planted, so it was fair game.

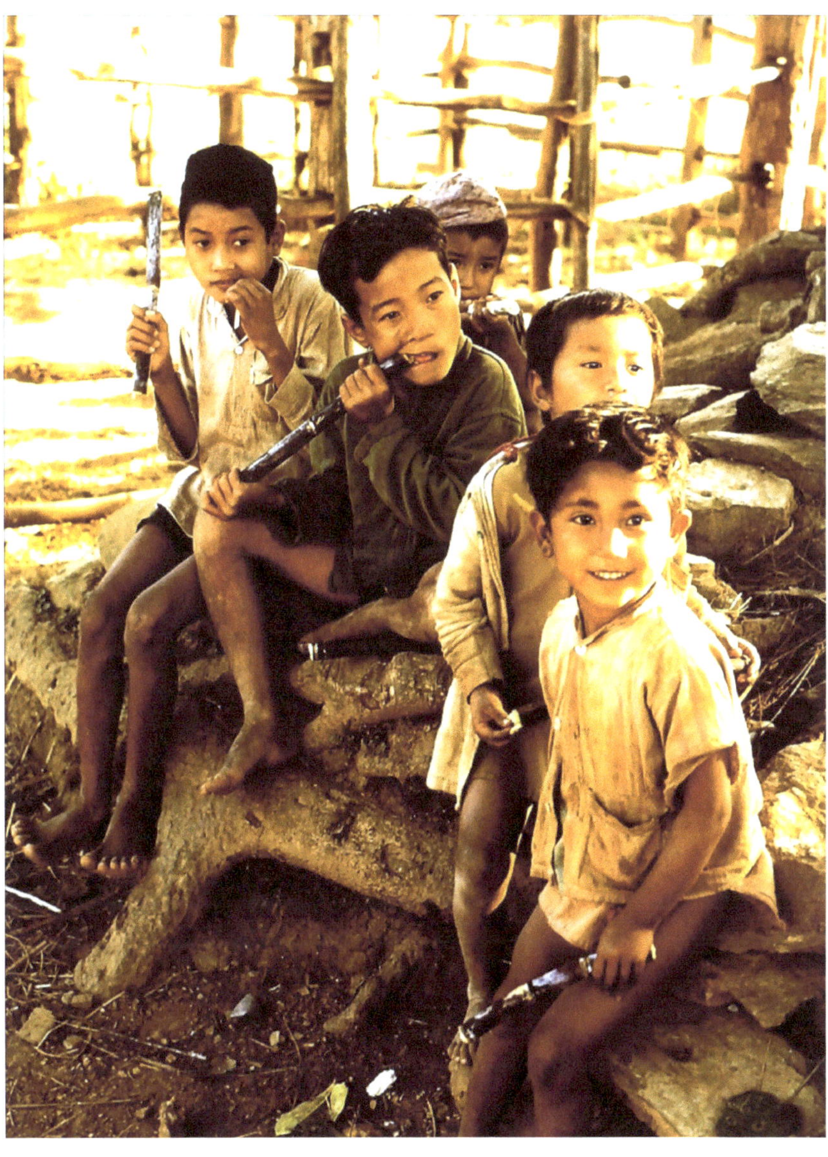

Devi Lal (green jacket) and the boys. The "jail" is in the background.

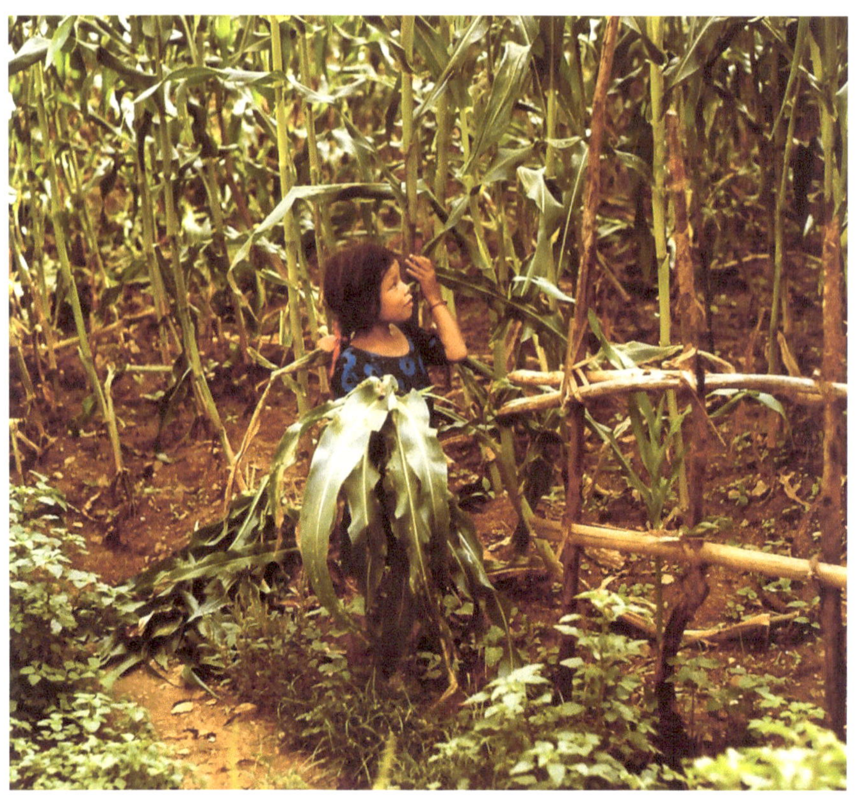

Older children pick leaves and branches to feed to a family's live-stock during the dry season.

September 27, 1973

It was bound to happen sooner or later I suppose. Me 'en the boys (and I do mean boys) were playing a lively game of 21 the other night. It happened that Devi Lal brought along his little seven month old sister. Little kids here are taken care of by older brothers and sisters much of the day. They go everywhere and are as tough as knots. Devi Lal loves to take care of her and does a good job. He's a real big brother.

But when I saw the kid I thought she looked a little too jolly, a little too contented, like she had just been fed. You know, that type of look. Perhaps I should have said something then. Anyway, he sat her on the bed, on my down sleeping bag. She liked that, and immediately smiled, squealed and began to enjoy herself.

So we got the game going and had a high time of it. We each started with fifteen kernels of corn and before long I was out. That was O.K. since the game had gone on long enough. The little one had become quiet long before, so Devi Lal took her home to "ama."

When all had left, I discovered why the little tyke had been so quiet. Right in the middle of my sleeping bag was a big wet spot! Something like that is a very disconcerting thing to discover a few minutes before going to bed. But, after a while in Nepal, a person learns to take such natural events in stride. Who can be mad at little innocent babes, even those that run around with no pants, and mess all over your sleeping bag?

I've since told Devi Lal not to bring her into my room. I took all his corn away too.

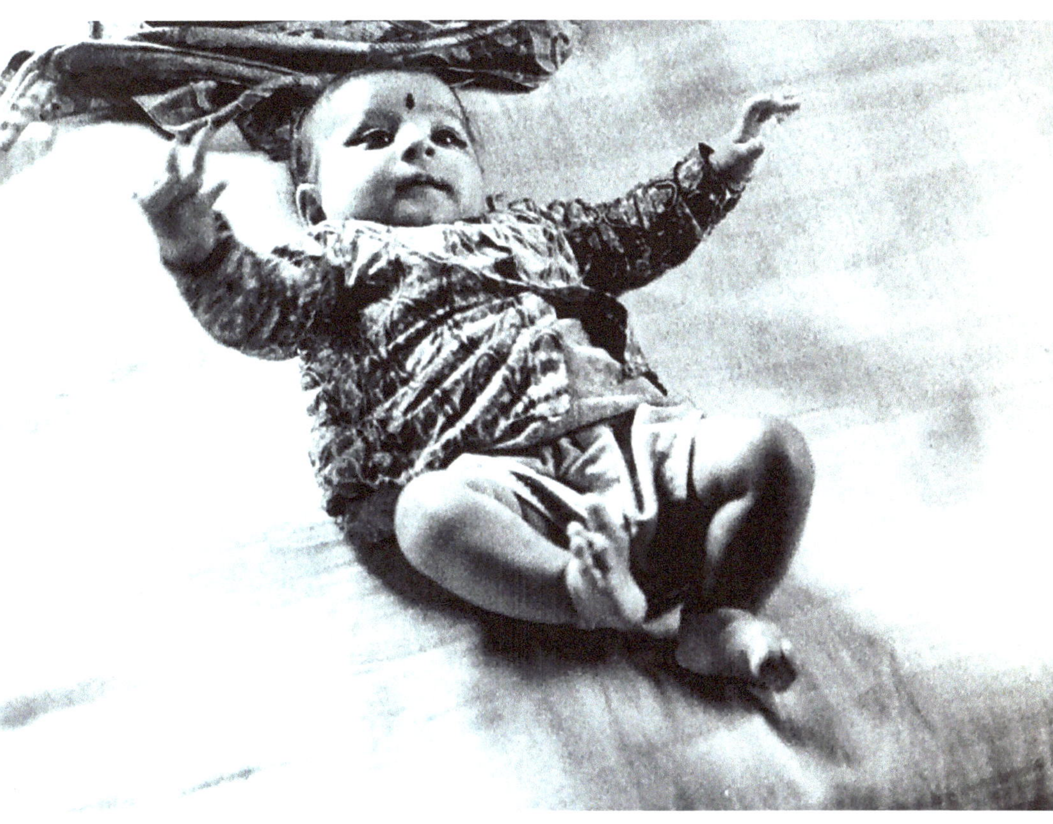

Baby with red rouge "tika" mark on her forehead

Damaulie, May 28, 1973

School will be out soon. That's a good thing, too. It's impossible to teach when it rains, and that's quite frequently now. Besides the fact that there's no roof to speak of, and the only half protected classroom fell to pieces during a real hummer of a storm three or four weeks ago, half the kids don't show up if it's raining. Course, I don't blame them. I nearly get stuck in the red clay in the short distance I walk to school. I can imagine what the barthos are like that some of these kids must walk on for two hours to reach school.

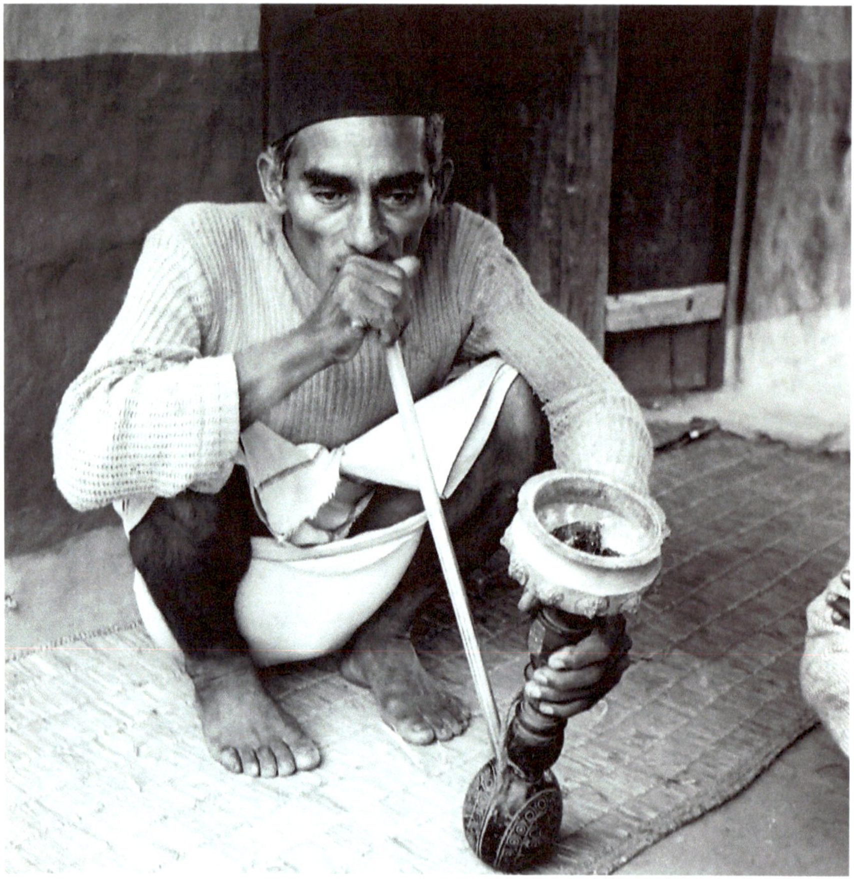

As if respiratory problems weren't bad enough due to cooking fires in each home, smoking tobacco (or other vegetable matter) using a water filled "hookah" is also common. The top of the device is a clay bowl having a porous base into which hot coals and the drug of choice are placed. The remainder of the hookah is made of wood and can be ornately carved.

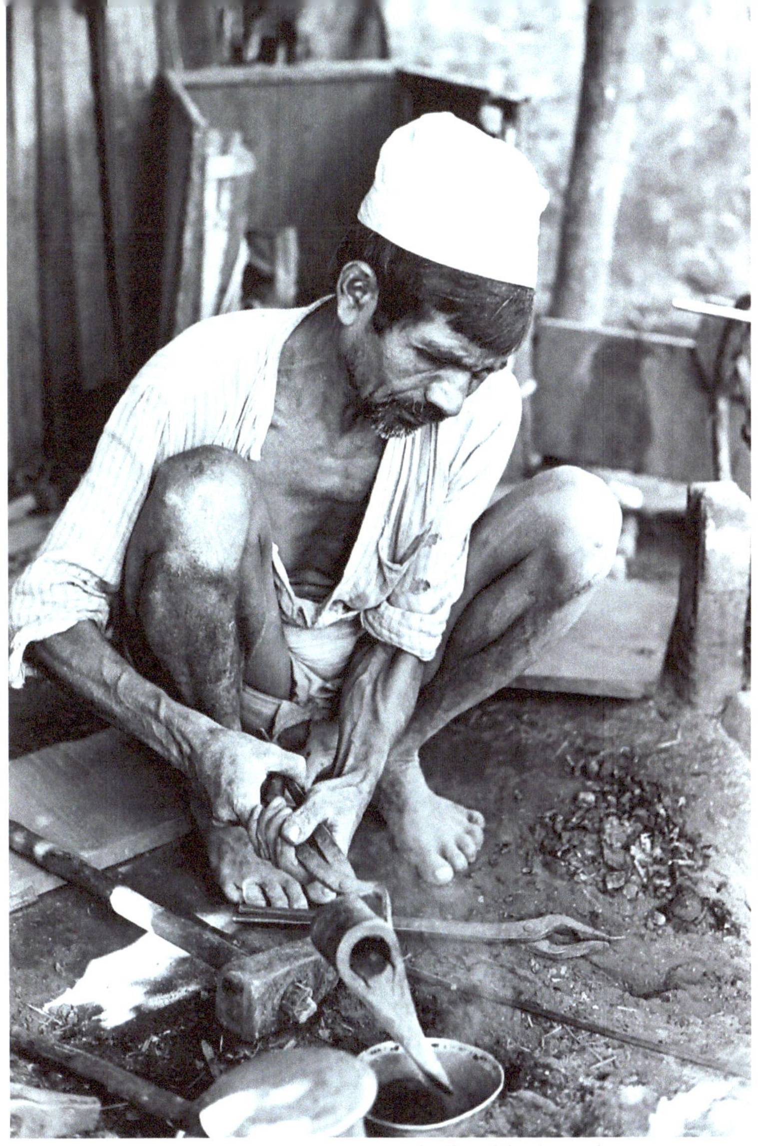

"sharky" or blacksmith

Damaulie, June 12, 1973

No matter how small the village you can usually find a tailor. These guys are quite talented using a small hand cranked sewing machine set on the dirt floor in front of them. If you're thinking of a new suit, you first buy your material at a cloth pasaul. Whatever material is left over goes to the tailor. One volunteer thought five yards would be plenty for a dress, but it still ended a little skimpy. The next week she saw the tailor's two girls running around in dresses with the same print pattern as hers!

Sometimes you see suits made from the end of a roll of cloth. The mill prints it's name and trademark on the last few feet of each bolt. But nothing is wasted. These become Saturday morning bargains for the villagers. The result is a jaunty little guy with a spiffy new suit. Down one sleeve or across the back is stamped, "SHREE BADHRA MILLS, suitings and yard goods, 100% cotton."

But who cares? One good rain shower and it will lose one size, along with the unwanted advertisement.

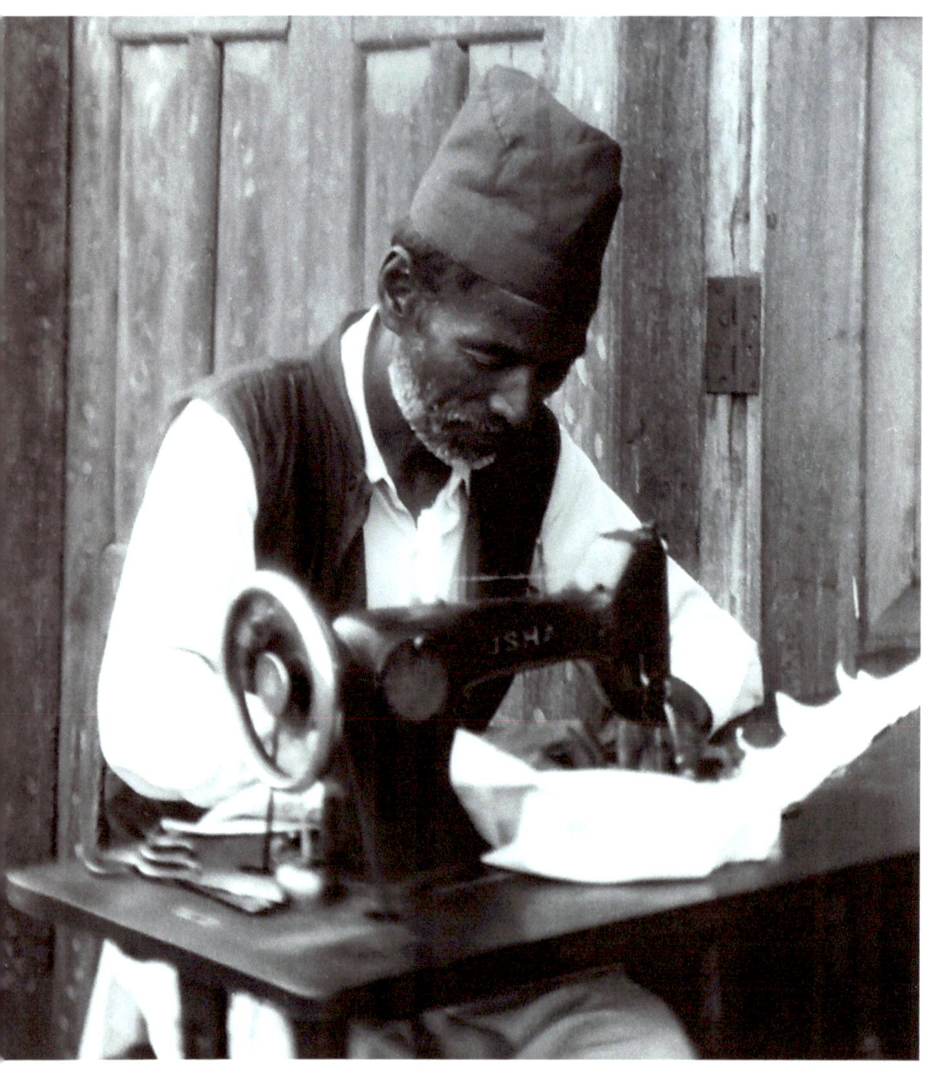

The national headdress for males, and a steady seller for local tailors, is the "topi".

sewing a coin purse

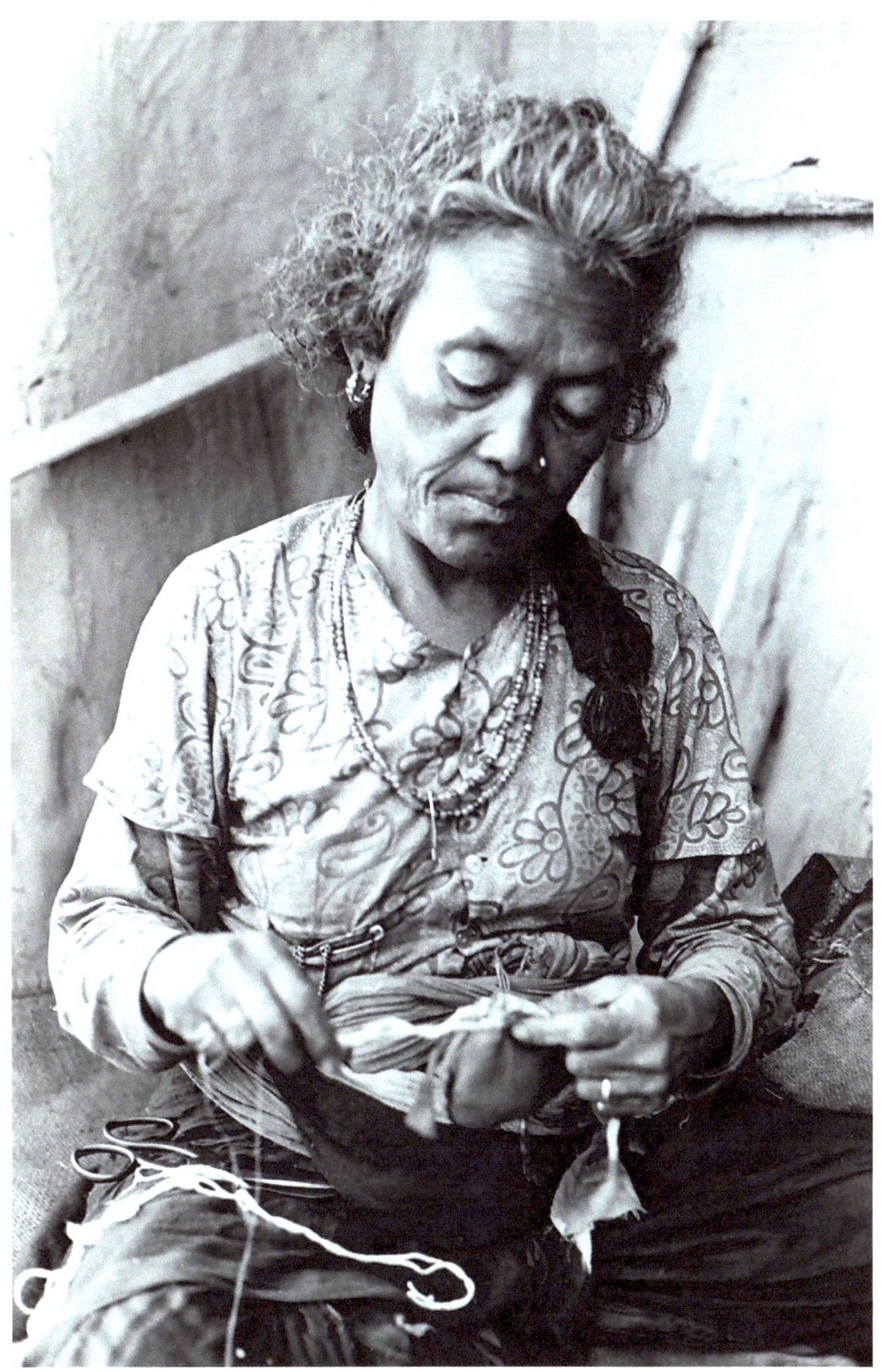

potter and son

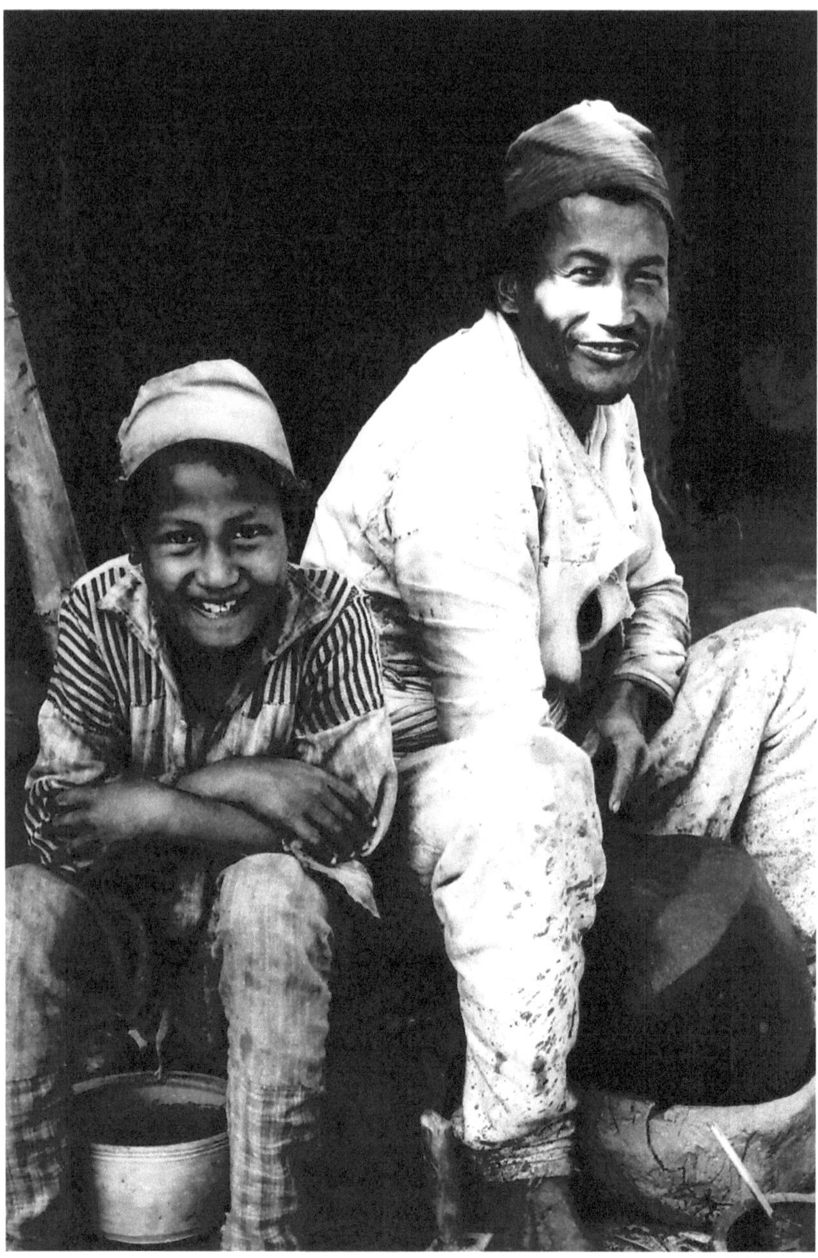

A family of potters came to our area and stayed for several weeks, making mostly standard Nepalese water pots from a clay deposit along the river. I had them make me about 10 feet of chimney flue as a special order. It's now installed and works great on my cooking stove, much to the amazement of the locals.

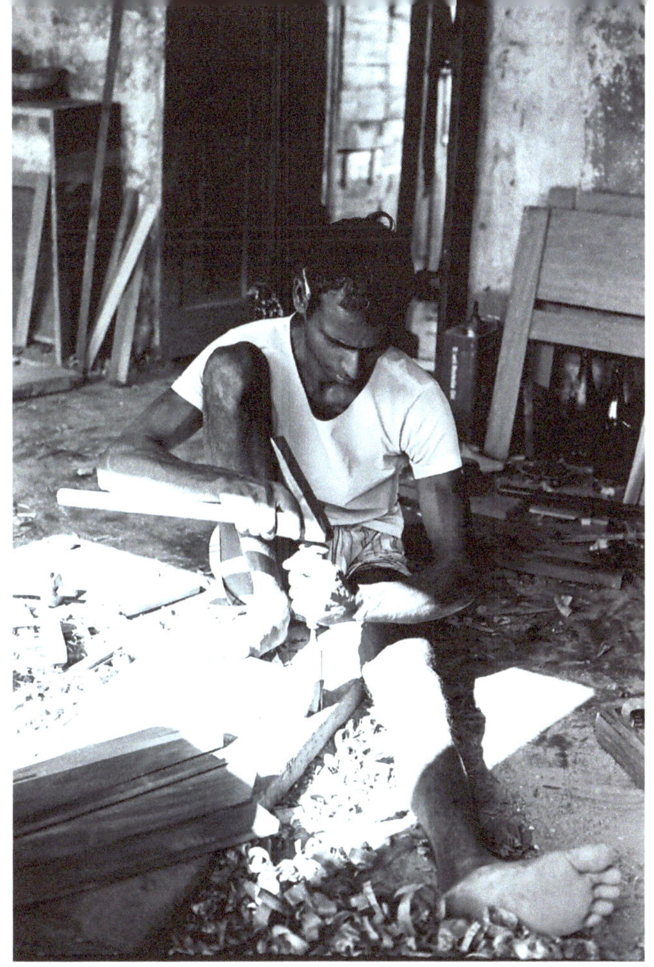

Carpenter

Damaulie, October 21, 1973

I want you to know I am a benefactor of the arts. A little aspiring virtuoso and his apprentice came by yesterday forenoon. He had a homemade fiddle. They sat in front of my door to play and sing. Afterward I gave each a rupee.

Musicians in Nepal have a little different approach to the art from those in the west. It is essentially begging. First you get what money you can in spontaneous donations from the crowd, moved as they are to the heights of rapture by the strains. Then you zero in on any gullible looking patron and chant a few lines for his or her special benefit in hopes of an extra handout.

However, I was able to keep the shirt on my back after this benefit performance. I thought the one rupee was pretty good earnings, for a musician that is.

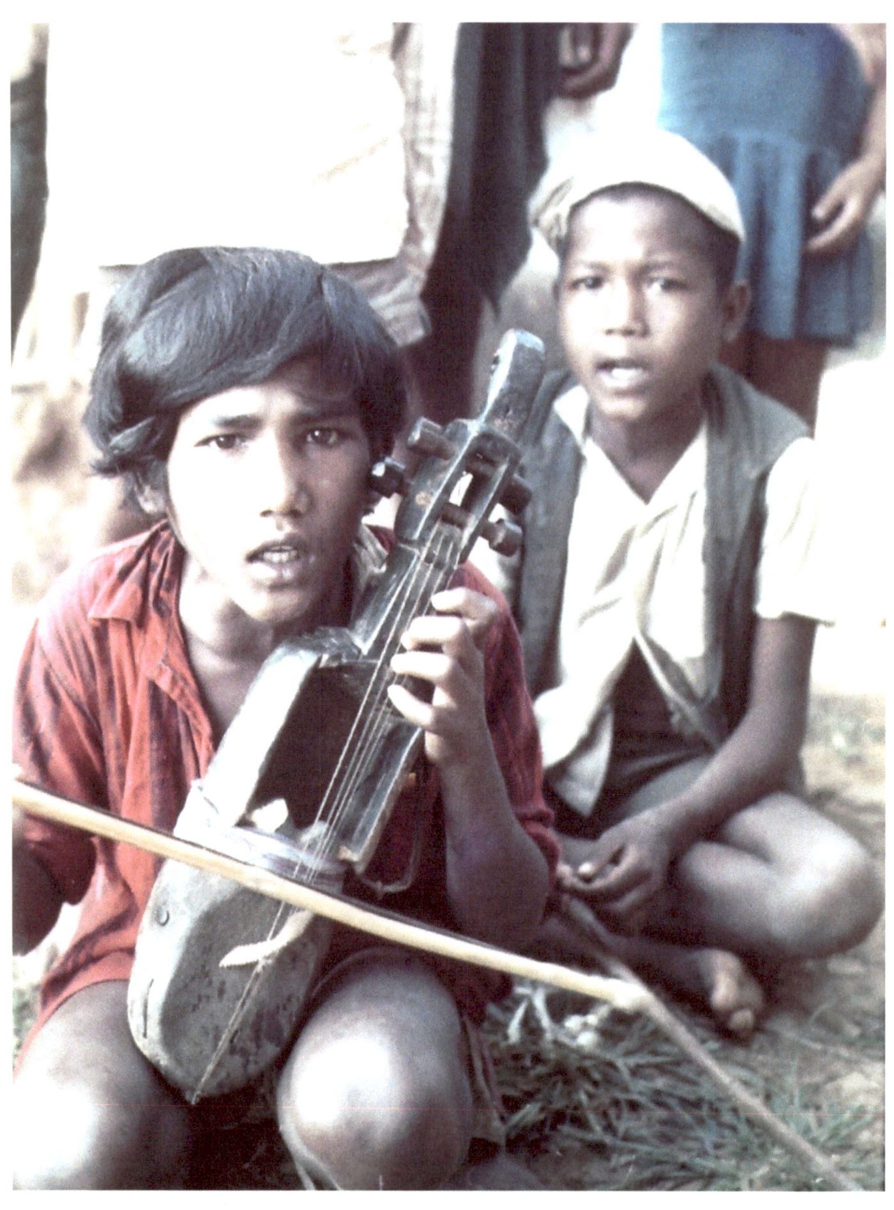

musicians

Damaulie, November 3, 1973

Nepalese by and large have excellent night vision. Walking after dark with only the moon or less for illumination, they can cross the rice paddies on narrow six inch wide dikes between fields with nary a problem,. Meanwhile, I'm falling, flailing and fumbling, and often end up straddling the dike. I guess years of television and indoor lights don't help one's night vision.

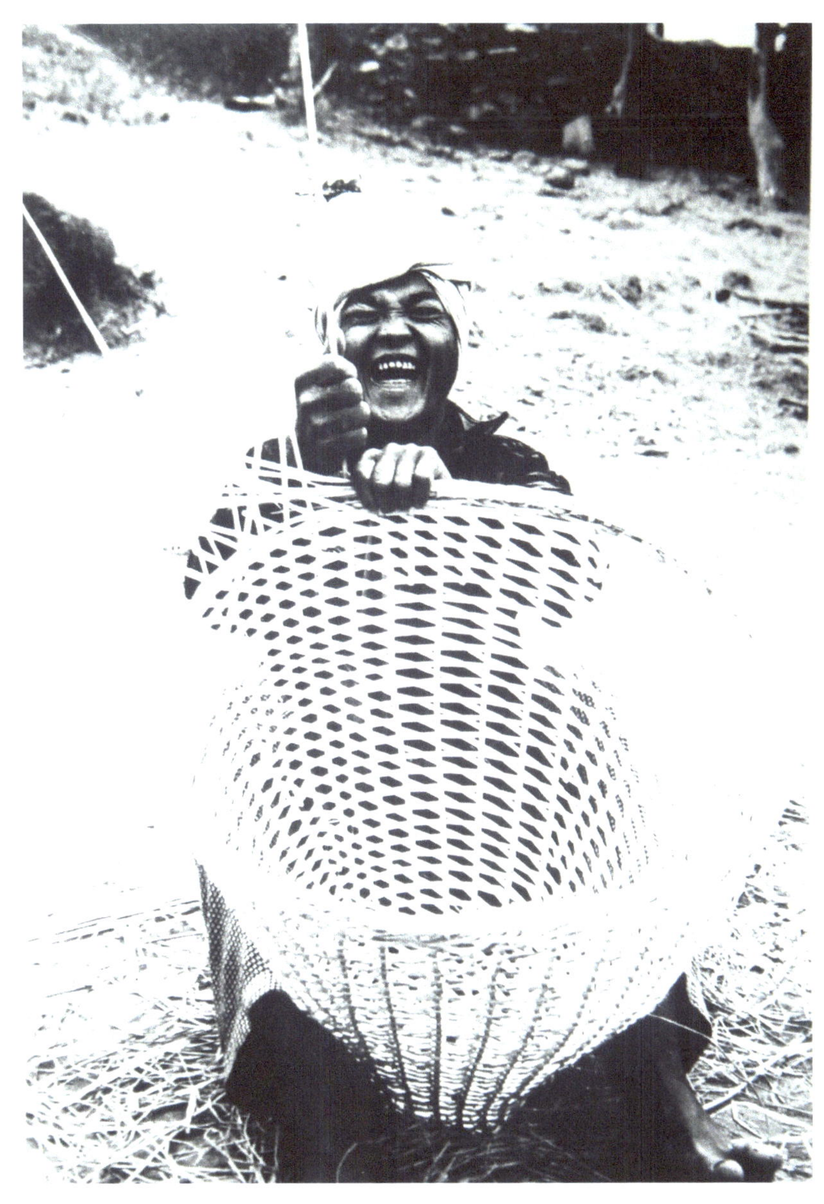

a basket weaver

December 8, 1973

Another volunteer stopped by and left four packages that were supposed to go to Chuck, my neighbor about ten miles west along the road in the village to Tharphu. So, I packed them off and planned to spend the night at Chuck's. With all the goodies I didn't feel there would be a need to rush right back to Damaulie.

It so happened that one box said, "Love, Mom, Dad and Linda." It was a ten pound box of Keebler® cookies fresh from the factory. Chuck said he had heard of Mom and Dad, but couldn't reckon right off where Linda fit in. It was quite a problem, I'll tell you, especially after we noticed the small letters: To Will W…...

I had a sudden strong recollection that Will had left these parts. We both sat and watched that virgin box of cookies. What a temptation to place in the hands of two all American, lonesome young men. And with the monsoon coming in just another two months, that luscious white box would be all but ravished by ants and soggy weather. Both of us saw clearly what our duty to this innocent lost orphan should be. When Chuck said he had an even stronger recollection that Will had long since left, and knew it was so, and would most nearly take an oath on it, why is was good enough convincing testimony for me. I think I liked the little windmills covered with almonds the best, though it's hard to tell.

Chuck was expecting a box with some new Levi's too, but they never showed up. Maybe Will? No, it was probably just lost, or stolen. A lot of that happens over here. I think it's the Indians.

Damaulie, December 5, 1973

During the dry winter months, cattle are highly stressed and many succumb. Vultures are considered unclean because they eat carcasses, including those of cows that have dropped by the wayside. In Kathmandu, cows, which don't seem to belong to any particular owner, wander the streets searching for anything to eat. Cardboard boxes and newspapers often provide the only available forage. It's not uncommon to see a ragged looking cow beside the street contentedly chewing on a section of the Hindustan Times. Some time ago, the Swiss helped establish a modern dairy operation and are striving to improve the local herds. I don't know how they handle the delicate problem of culling those cattle that no longer are capable of prime milk production.

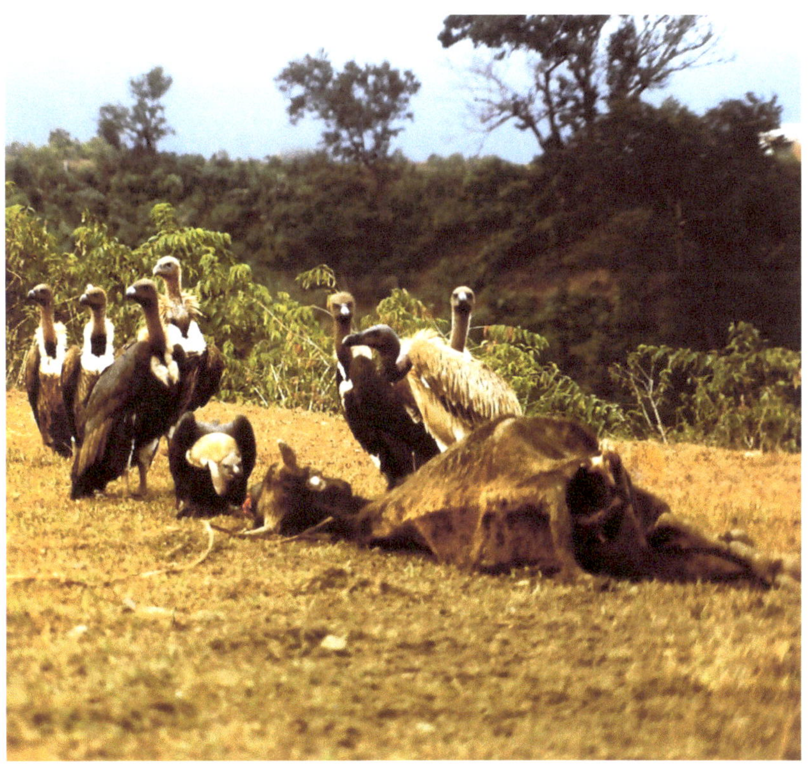

the end for all holy cows

Damaulie, January 12, 1974

Today is Freedom Day. Everyone, students, police, government officials, paraded around the big bazaar. We held up a few buses going to Kathmandu and shouted how great it was to live under the benign rule of the King. I became a little carried away with the excitement and bought a pack of firecrackers. On the second pass roun' the bazaar I let 'em rip. But I guess some of the government people were a mite nervous. The Chief of Police told me to cool it. It seems that some subjects don't celebrate Freedom Day in the same high spirits. Assassinations occur with alarming regularity. As a result, loud noises don't set too well with the big wigs.

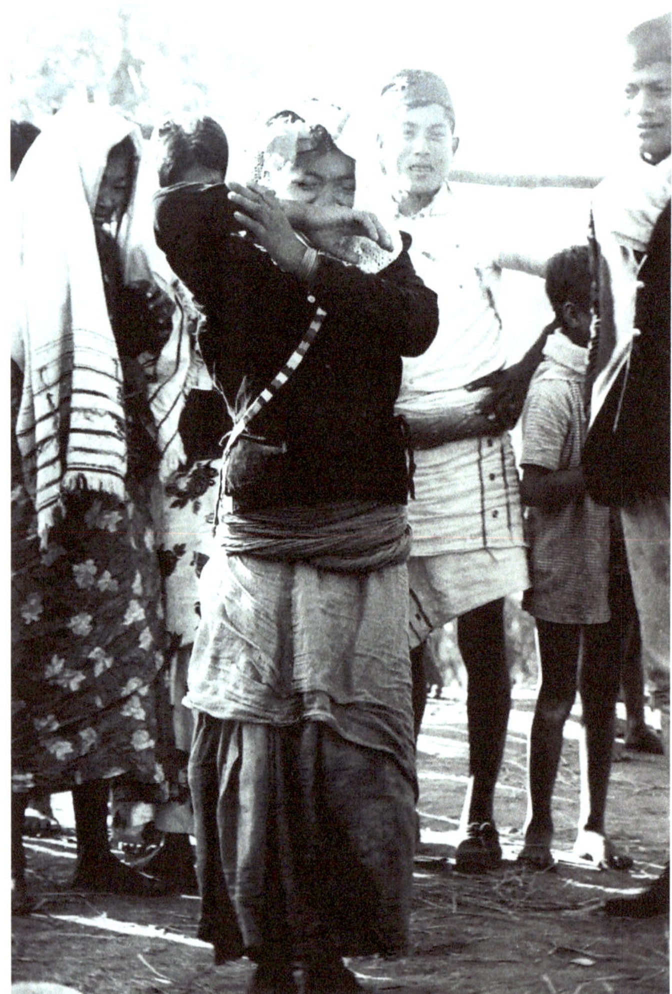

wedding party

Damaulie, February 9, 1974

This has been the month for weddings. Remember Nepalese months are about fifteen days off from ours. So we are about to the end of Magh, one of the six months of the year propitious enough for the risky business of weddings. I attended one last weekend, a subdued affair because it was a Brahmin couple. The bride was a sister of one of the teachers at school, and he gave me a special invitation to attend. We had to walk about three hours to his home village. I was almost bowled over while fording a river during the hike. We finally arrived about "bhat" time, ten o'clock in the morning.

Friends and relatives started dropping by the house later that afternoon. There was stuff to munch on: corn and rice flower breads, some very sweet. About dark, the procession came bringing the groom. Several musicians led the pack with drums, horns and symbols. They'd stop every few minutes and let rip with a chorus of variegated sounds. The groom was carried in a sling beneath a long pole carried by two men. He looked for all the world like a scared raccoon and clung securely to this pole to the merriment of all.

At the bride's house, an altar had been constructed with four banana stalks and bamboo leaves. It was decorated with colored flowers, threads and red cloth to form a square. The groom's father and older brothers sat next to the altar and ate "bhat" prepared by the bride's mother. Meanwhile, the band was really humming away at all those old-time Nepalese favorites, and all the neighbors came over to join in the festivities.

Soon, the bride made her appearance. She wore a new red sari, with sequins and jewels in her hair, and gold earrings and bracelet. Her face was covered with a veil and she was carried to a seat beside the groom at the altar. Here they repeated verses from sacred Hindu writings led by a Brahmin "guru" especially invited to the wedding for this purpose. After the vows, the couple gave special "pujha" blessings for each other and all assembled, and bestowed red powder tika marks on everyone's foreheads. Finally, the groom sprinkled red powder in the bride's hair, the sign of a married woman in Nepal, and she did the same to him in return.

All the guns went off, and the dogs howled as the 200 or so people present moved towards a large vacant rice field for the feast. I had wondered about a little hut made of branches and leaves in one corner of the field after arriving earlier in the day. Several women were there, preparing to cook rice and vegetables in four large copper kettles each holding about ten gallons.

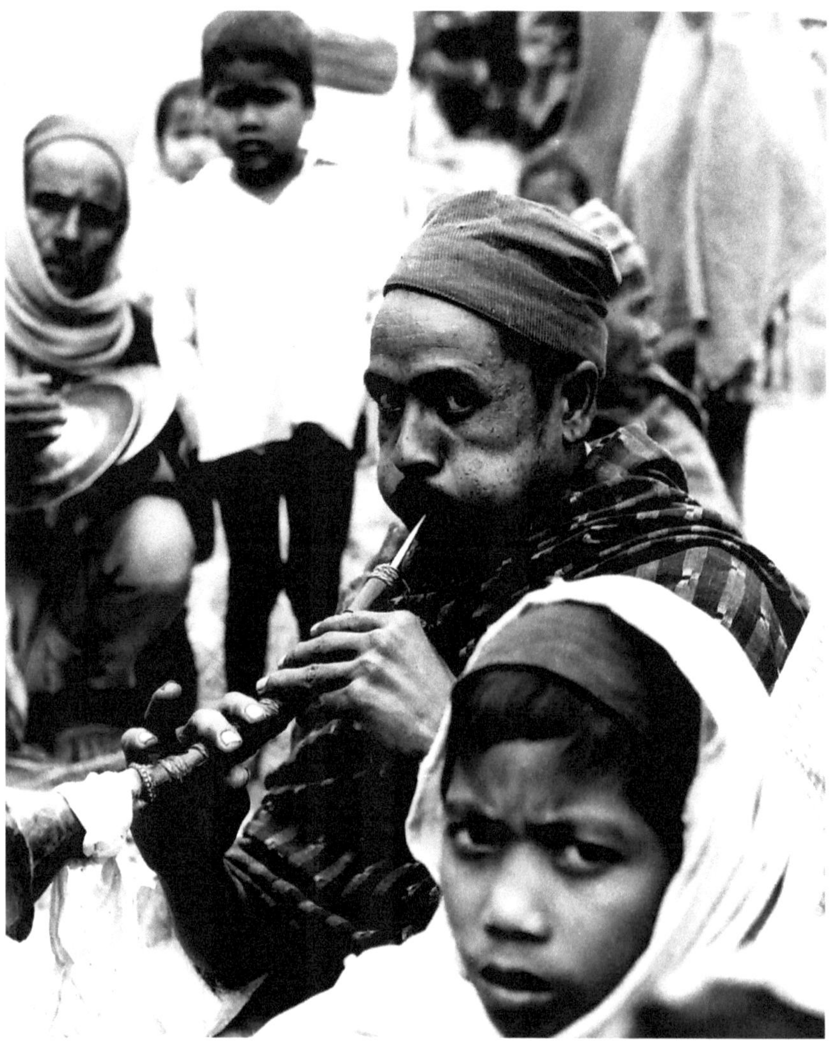

solo horn

I walked over to give a big, mid-western, "howdy," but was rebuffed by their rude behavior. Each cook turned her face from me and practically ran away! I was rescued from my difficult situation by one of the small fry observing me. He led me safely away from the sacred cooking area.

The women had gotten over their earlier fright and were ready to feed the mob with tubs full of rice and curried vegetables. We ate from leaf plates, the original disposable picnic service. There were rice with lentils, sugar, ghee (water buffalo butter) yogurt, milk and several vegetables, plus all sorts of pickles, relishes, and other stuff. Since it was dark, I didn't know what anything was, but just kept on eating. My host was forbidden to eat anything until the following morning. He was the oldest brother of the bride and since their father had passed on, he had to perform some of the parts of the ceremony. His head was shaved earlier in the day and now he wore a single white loin cloth called a "lungi." I offered to sneak him some food on the side, but he declined, walking instead among the guests, serving food and seeing that all were cared for.

After dinner, sleeping quarters were found for everyone. The band and overflow crowd ended up in the "bissee" stall. I was shown a spot upstairs and was soon fast asleep only to be awakened at one o'clock in time for the sacred "feet washing" ceremony. My genial host didn't want me to miss any of the excitement! The ceremony took place downstairs in the cooking room. I sleepily climbed down the notched pole used for a stairway, and looked into the crowded room. The bride, with a veil still covering her face, and the groom sat in the middle of the room. My host gave me a leaf with sacred rice and red powder. He told me to use it to place a tika on their foreheads, and to give at this time any money I felt like giving.

Money! My wallet was still upstairs! By now, I was into the room with the little leaf full of powder, and decided to make a good show of it in spite of the money problem. Perhaps I could make it up later. I sprinkled the powder and rice as expertly as I thought a non-Hindu could, and bowed once or twice. I appeared to not notice the small mound of coins and notes at their feet, but backed out of the room and found my way upstairs to bed again.

About five o'clock in the morning, the band let all know that they were still a viable group and the shindig dragged itself to its feet. The musicians had gotten into the mad passion of creativity and were giving this number all they had. Actually, the whole bunch could only command two notes between themselves. While the horn player concentrated as best he could on those, the two drummers and cymbal player threw in a run now and then to add spice to the whole thing.

I climbed downstairs and discovered the bride and groom seated outside before the altar with a fire before them for warmth. The bride had fallen asleep and was propped against her maid of honor. The worst was now past. Those who didn't have the opportunity earlier, now gave their tika marks. I found my wallet and dug out the illusive rupee from last evening.

The groom's side of the family engaged the bride's side in a friendly contest of verse. Each chanted a verse or riddle to the other side, and they in turn answered in like verse. This lasted for several hours with lots of laughter. Finally, the pole sling was brought to the altar. This time the bride would be carried to the groom's house.

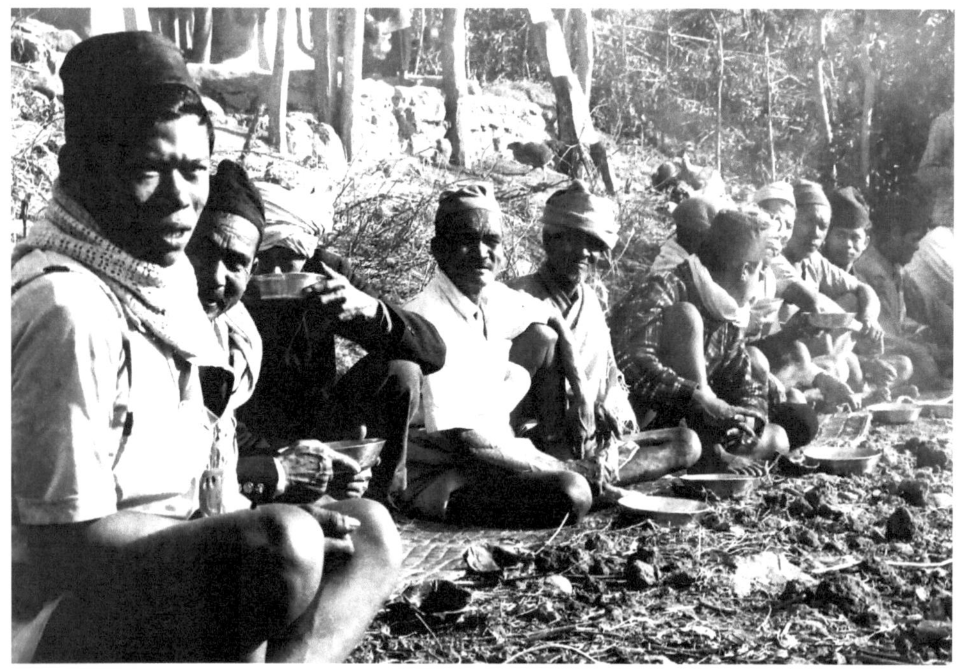

the feast

My host picked her up and carried her three times around the altar and placed her in the sling. She was wrapped in red and the sling was covered so nobody could see her. Then, band in the lead, all moved off to the groom's house for another day of the same festivities.

My host was eating once again. He told me he could not accompany the procession to the groom's house. In fact, he could not go to the new couple's house until after the first child was born. Such was the custom. It provided a good excuse for me to not accompany the group for the second day of celebration. Things at the bride's old house soon got back to normal after the crowd had left. After a good morning meal of bhat, I started back to Damaulie.

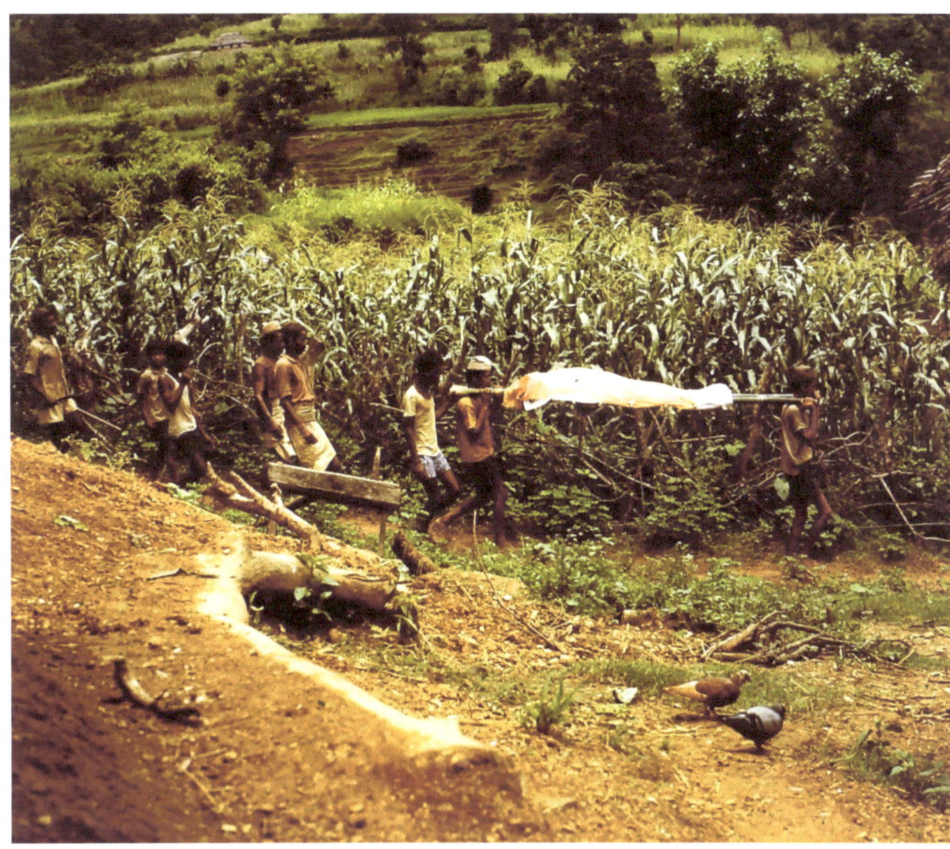

a funeral procession. Bodies are carried to the nearest river and burned. This custom ruins innumerable good swimming holes.

Hear the drums!
Across the night a happy sound.
In that circle each glowing face
Knows the thoughts of every race;
Hopes for joy, peace and cheer,
Love and brotherhood, free from fear.

Hear the drums!
Oh, a dolesome tone to tell all ears
One life is gone; a funeral nears.
And on each mourning follower's brow,
Perturbed thought queries somehow,
Is this all life should mean?

Hear the drums!
Look! A wedding draws near.
A boisterous clan, I wish you'd seen,
Yet in each breast was found man's dream.
For length of life, care when weak,
Success, honor; goals all men seek.

A "Yogi" or Hindu holy man

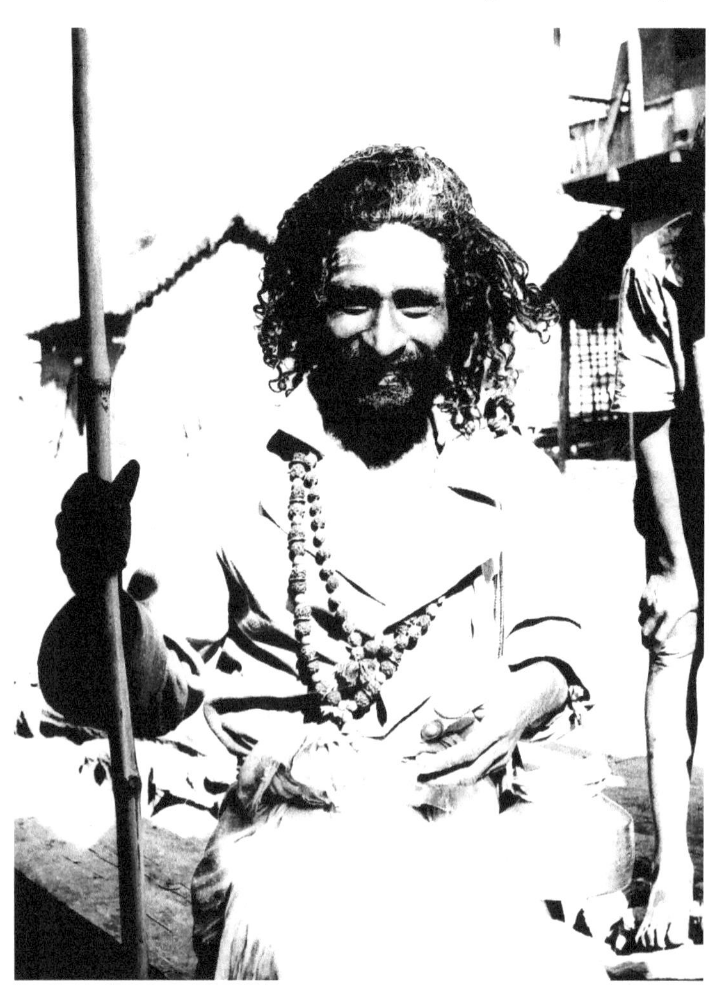

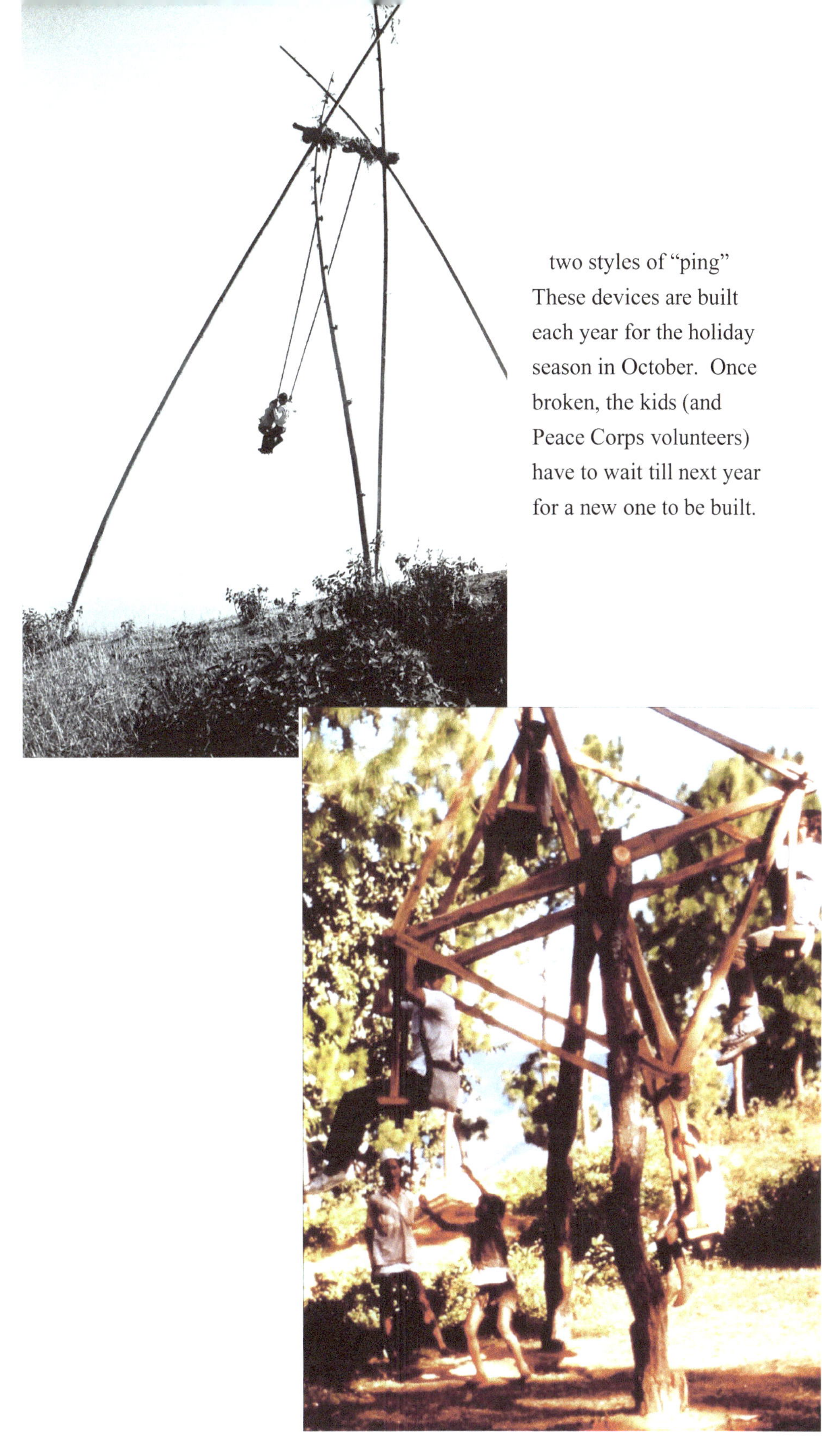

two styles of "ping"
These devices are built each year for the holiday season in October. Once broken, the kids (and Peace Corps volunteers) have to wait till next year for a new one to be built.

Damaulie, April 5, 1974

Every tree that has a green leaf has been stripped bare to provide green vegetation for the cows, bissee, and goats. Each evening the kids come down from the hillside carrying big bundles of cut branches on their backs. All of the trees close by look like telephone poles covered with nubs where each year's branches have been hacked off. The rest of the trees are shedding their leaves, making the whole area look about a hospitable as a dust bin. The trees don't even bother to turn color. Instead, they hold out as long as possible, and then give up and let fall to the ground their dried-out leaves. In a short time, new leaves appear, only to face the threat of the army of knives that attack every evening.

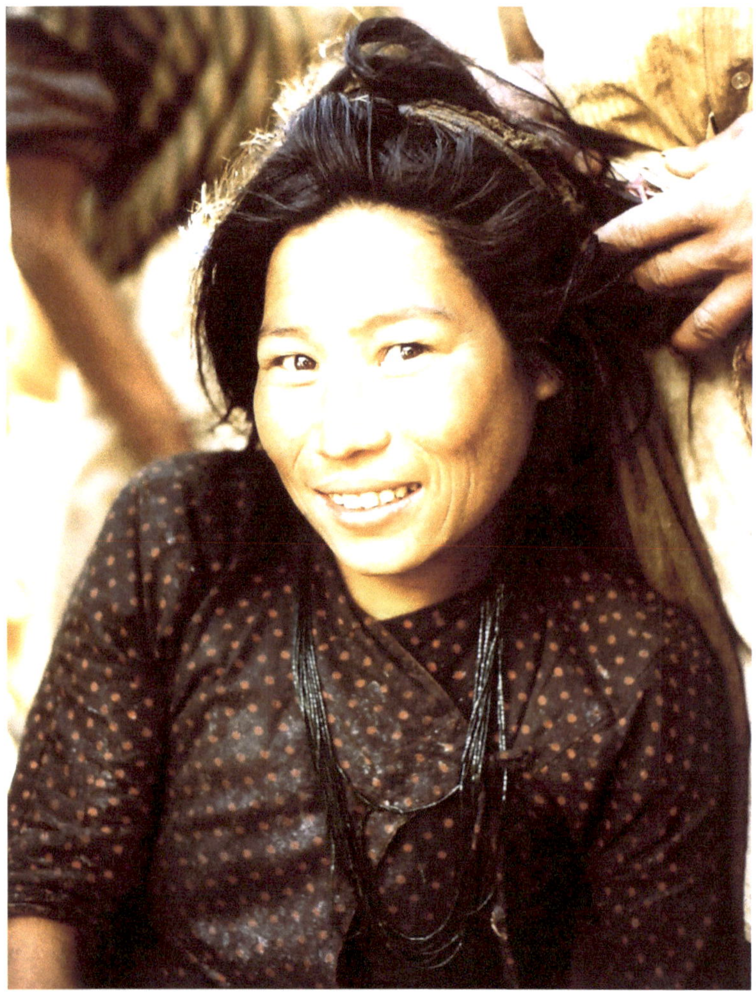

native dress

Damaulie, May 10, 1974

I went up north two weeks ago and brought back some 8mm movie equipment that another volunteer had left in his village after he returned home. The films, a projector, and a portable generator were sent from Germany as part of an educational experiment. They are quite interesting and informative, especially for those people who've had no chance to see foreign scenes and events. Now I'm a big hero about this area for showing these films in several evening shows. The best one I think is about Apollo 15. But, some of the villagers still just can't believe that men traveled to their god in a rocket.

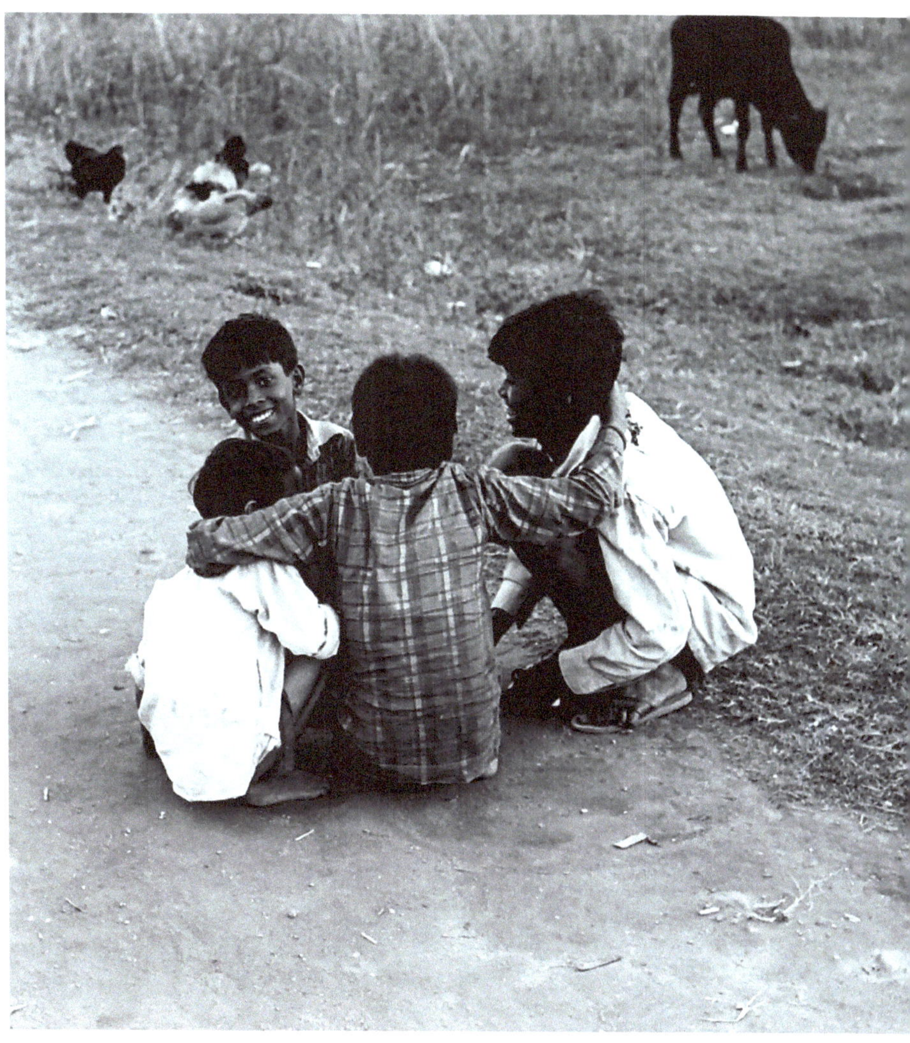

children beside the road

Damaulie, May 21, 1974

There aren't many dogs that are actual pets here. However, each village seems to possess a few thin and mangy strays. They dare not approach most adults for fear of being kicked or clubbed. The reason for their status as social pariahs is due to their useful but repugnant service of cleaning up after those who utilize the woods and fields surrounding a dwelling or village as natural lavatories. With no other reliable food source, the dogs survive by eating human excrement. The local mutts often takes keen notice of the various tots that run around without diapers to see if they might squat and leave something of interest.

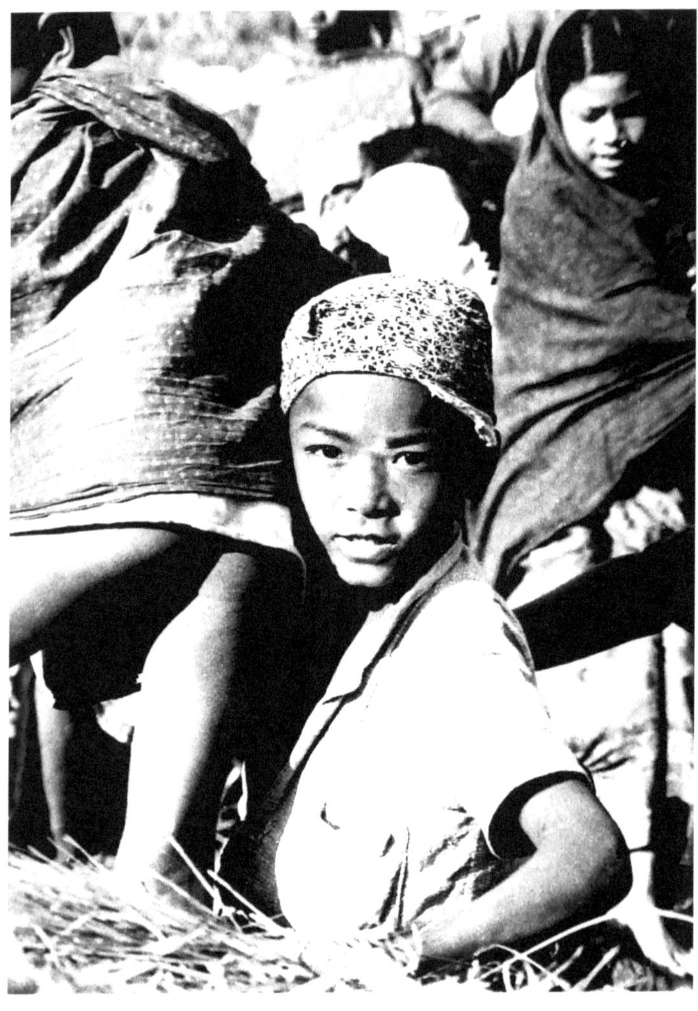

tykes usually go bare-bottomed for convenience

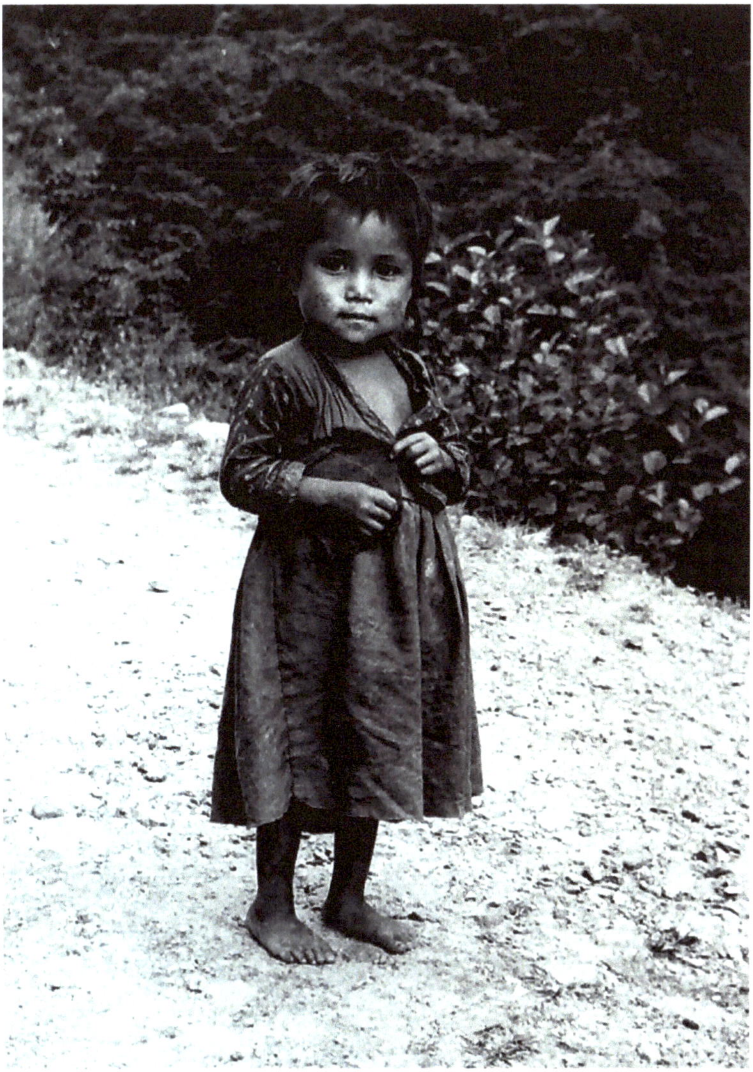

Damaulie, June 6, 1974

Devi Lal and I went fishing last week using a fish trap made from thin strips of bamboo. It looked like this:

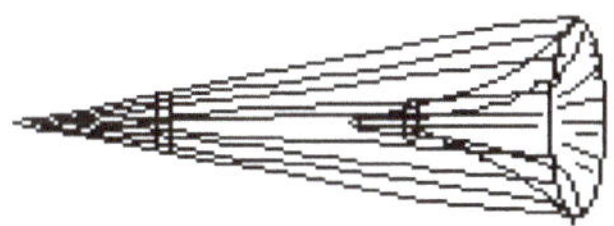

The fish go into the entrance but can't escape. To use the trap we first dug a shallow ditch next to the stream. The stream bed is very wide and the stream itself quite narrow because of the lack of rain.

So it was easy to divert a little water from the main stream into a channel of our own design. Then we made a place at the end of our channel to set the trap so that all the water and escaping fish must pass into the trap.

Our bait was sour corn mash from the local beer the villagers make mixed with manure to form a ball. This was the size of a grapefruit and kept the mash from floating away. We put that in a small hole scooped in middle of our channel. The fish (actually minnows by our standards) really went for the mash. After about an hour, hundreds of the unsuspecting little critters were nibbling at the dung ball. Then Devi Lal snuck up to the exit and quickly threw the trap into place, while I plugged the entrance with my big feet.

All the fish shot for the exit as soon as they knew the gig was up. But not one went into the trap! When they became packed together near the trap all started to jump and skip- right out of our channel and into the stream. I'll never forget seeing Devi Lal, the 12 year old fisherman, trying to hold the trap in place with one hand and grab with his free hand the slippery little escapees in front of him.

We're going to have a bigger trap made and try it again someday.

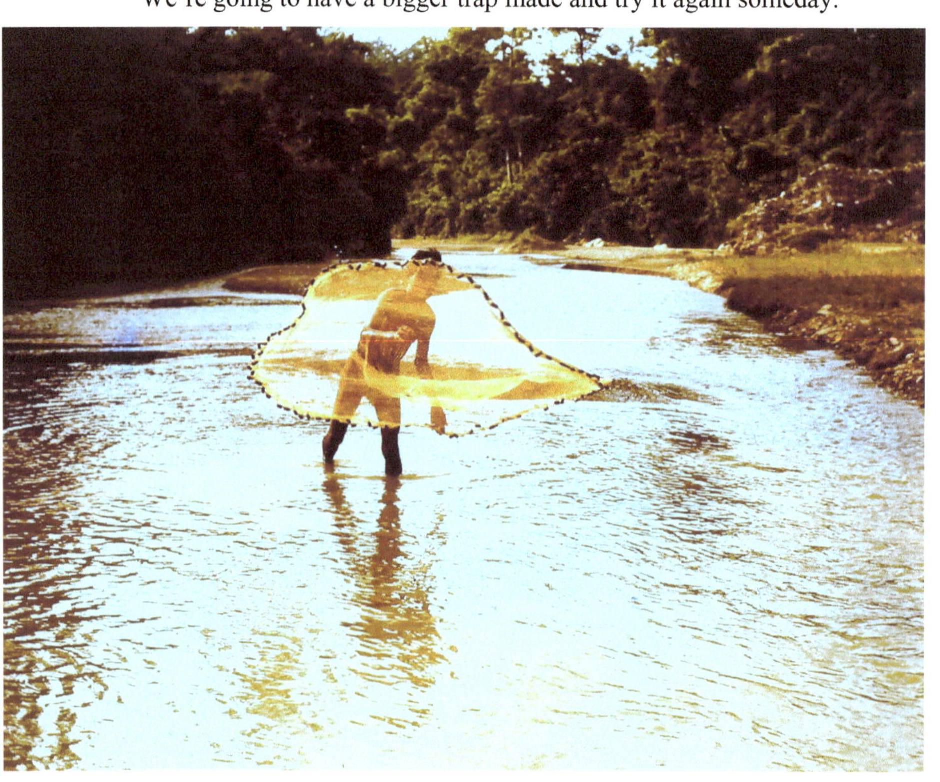

fishing for minnows

all in a line

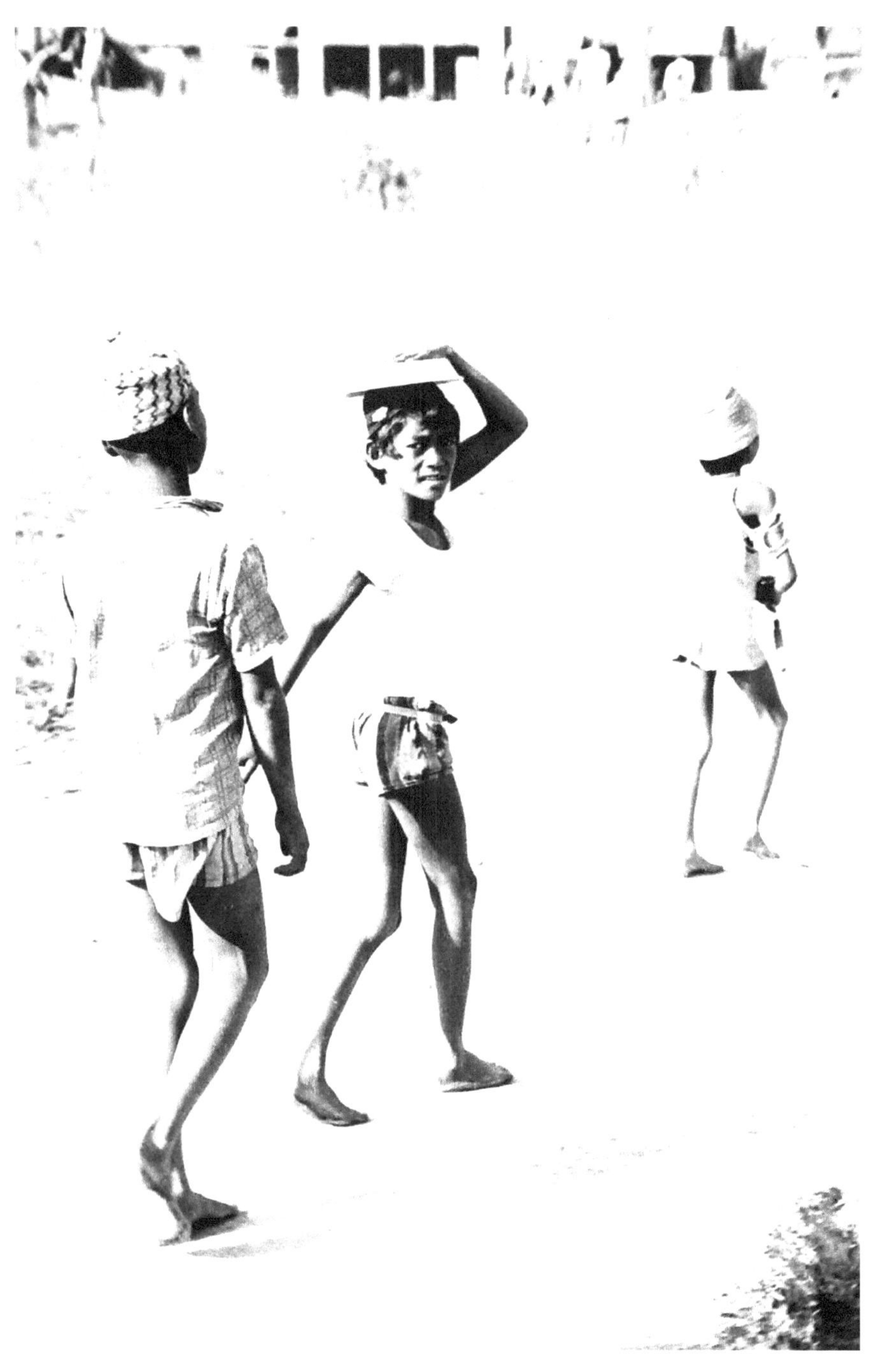

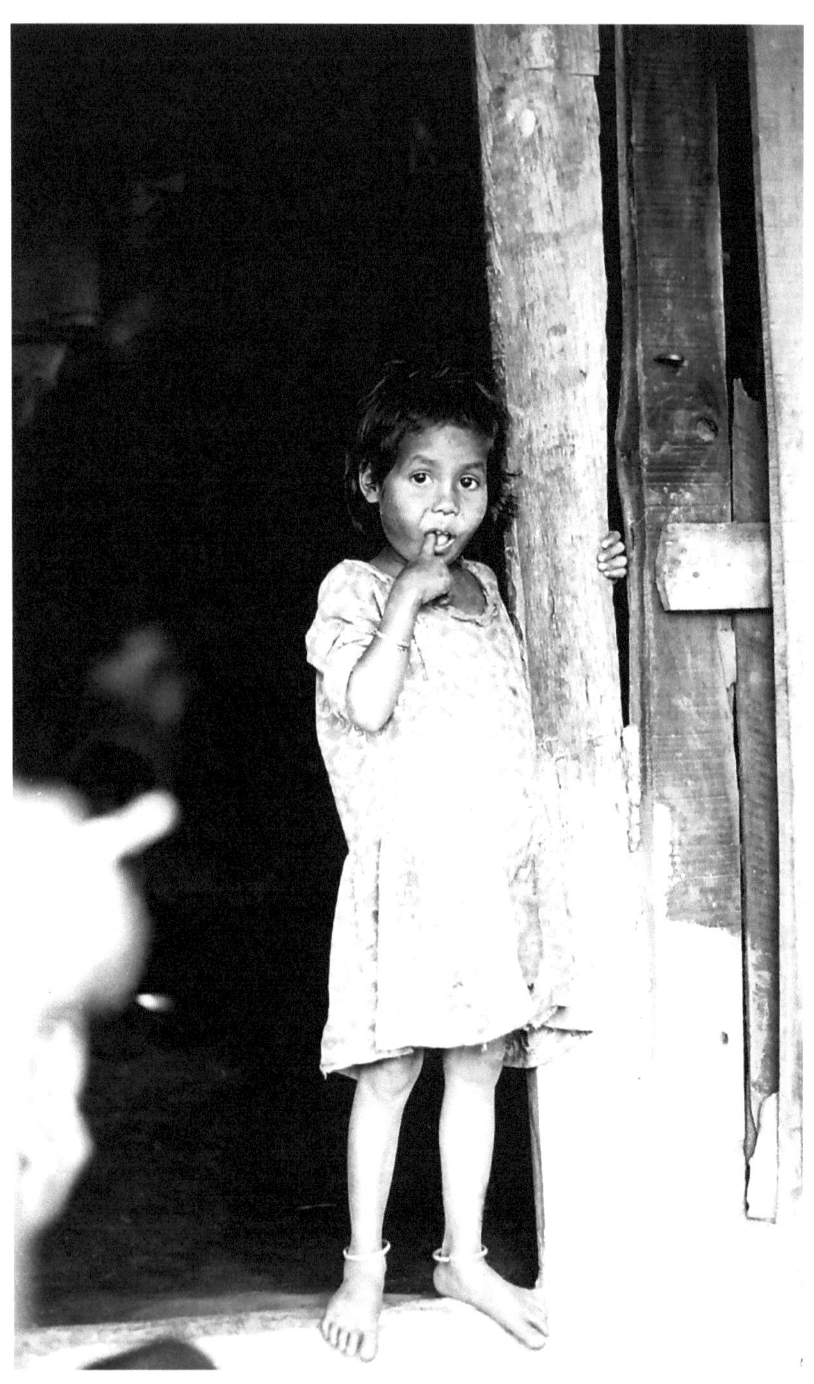

sharky's daughter

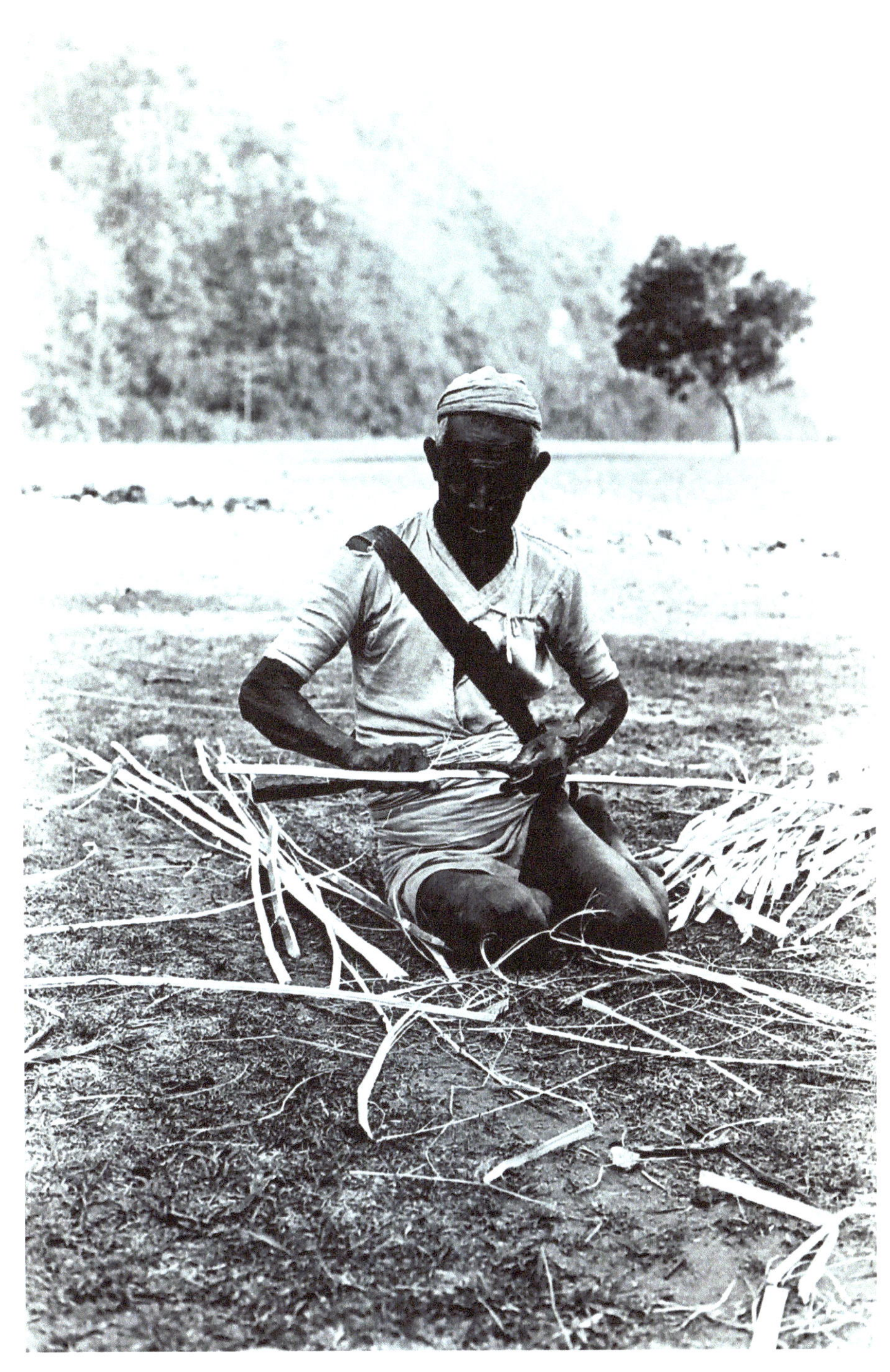

cutting bamboo with a hassia, a sickle shaped knife

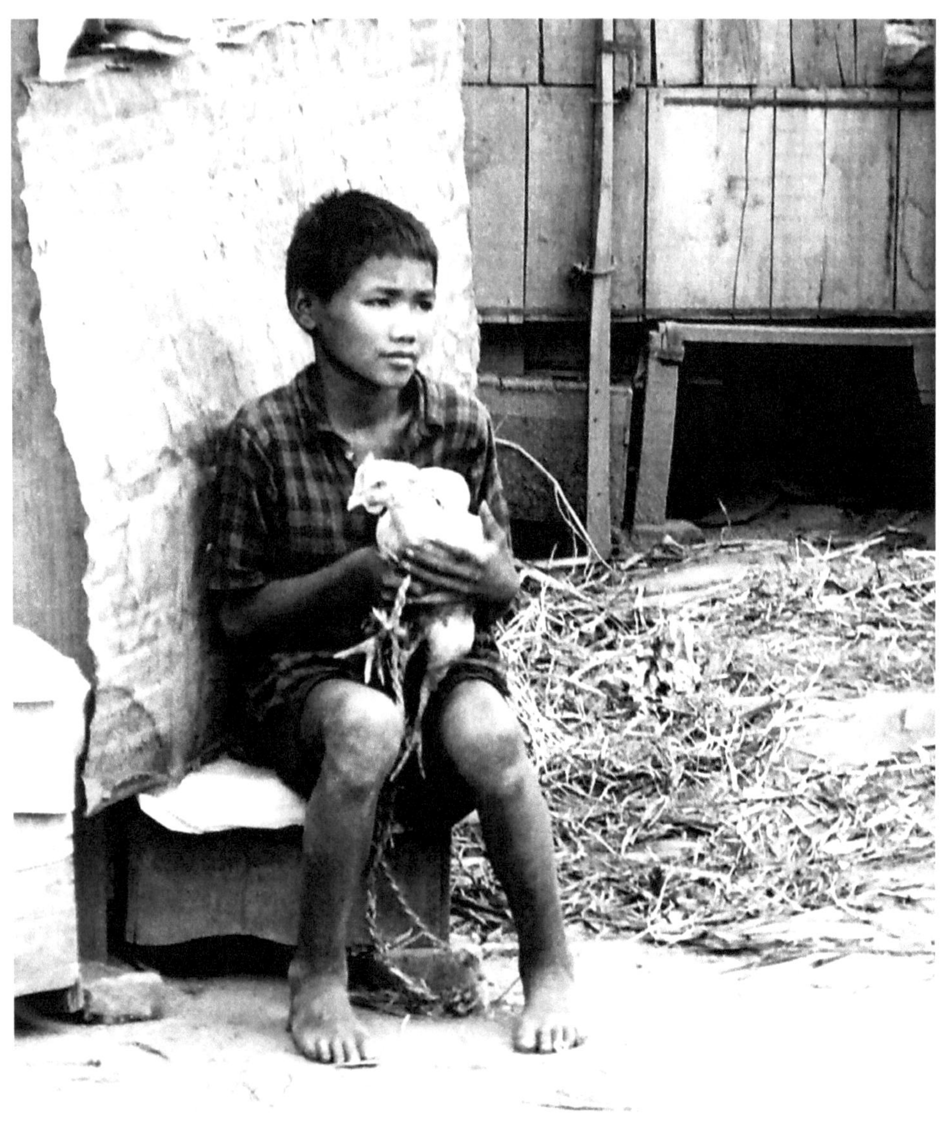

one chicken to sell

Kathmandu, October 18, 1974

Dear Ones All,

I left the village for the last time yesterday after saying good-bye all around. Many villagers gave most generously from their meager stores, an egg from one, a meal from another family. I was very moved by such selfless actions and asked many to not do anything special, but just say, "Nameste."

Didi insisted my last meal with them be special. So, that evening we had bhat and dahl, with two curried vegetables (spinach and potatoes), ghee (butter made from yogurt), yogurt and chicken. The next morning I left early to catch the bus over in the bazaar in the same spot where I'd arrived that dusty afternoon two years earlier. I said good-bye to the little family I'd known so well and walked into the misty morning across the "kets" (paddy fields) with Daju.

When we got to the river which was the last expanse to cross before coming to the road and my bus, he said, "Nameste," and asked me to stop on the other side of the stream and splash water back towards him three times. I can only guess that this was a blessing for their home and family or perhaps a promise to return. It was touching to me and important to him. After one last "Nameste," I turned and walked on to my waiting bus.

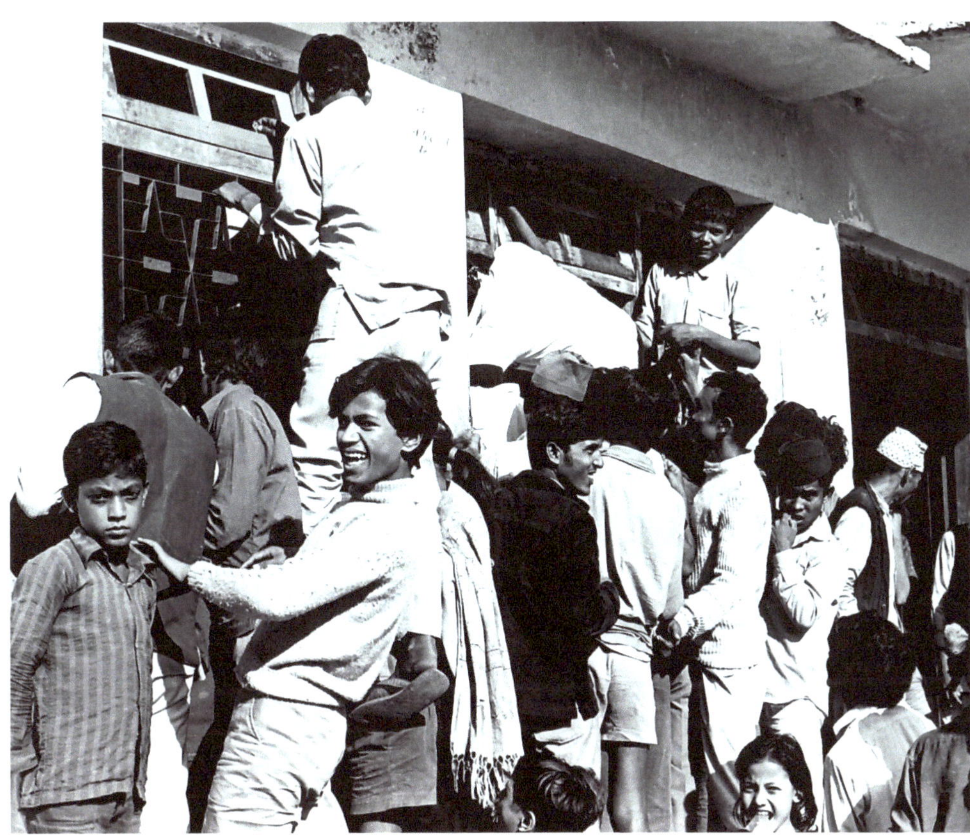

buying two up front at the Hindi cinema in Kathmandu

www.ingramcontent.com/pod-product-compliance
Lightning Source LLC
LaVergne TN
LVHW052258100826
845147LV00001B/79